Deborah Levy

Plays: 1

Pax; Clam; The B File;
Pushing the Prince into Denmark; Honey, Baby;
Macbeth – False Memories

Deborah Levy is a novelist and playwright. Her plays include *Pax* (Women's Theatre Company, UK and US tour, 1984); *Clam* (Oval House, 1985); *Heresies* (RSC, 1987); *The B File* (Chapter Arts, 1993); *Shiny Nylon* (The Women's Playhouse Trust, Royal Docks, 1994); *Honey, Baby* (laMama Theatre, Melbourne, 1995) and *Macbeth – False Memories* (Actors Touring Company, 1999). Her other published work includes short stories: *Ophelia and the Great Idea* (Vintage, 1985); poetry: *An Amorous Discourse in the Suburbs of Hell* (Vintage, 1990); five novels: *Beautiful Mutants* (Vintage, 1987), *Swallowing Geography* (Vintage, 1992), *The Unloved* (Vintage, 1994), and *Billy and Girl* (Bloomsbury, 1998). In 1999 Bookworks published *Diary of a Steak*, a meditation on celebrity and insanity. Screenplays include *Suburban Psycho* (a short film for BBC2, 1999) *and Circumstances of a Disappearance* (Loop Productions, 2000). From 1989–1991 Deborah Levy was Fellow in Creative Arts at Trinity College, Cambridge.

DEBORAH LEVY

Plays 1

Pax
Clam
The B File
Pushing the Prince into Denmark
Honey, Baby
Macbeth – False Memories

introduced by the author

Methuen

METHUEN CONTEMPORARY DRAMATISTS

Published by Methuen 2000

1 3 5 7 9 10 8 6 4 2

This collection first published in 2000 by Methuen Publishing Limited
215 Vauxhall Bridge Road, London SW1V 1EJ

Pax first published in *Plays by Women* vol. 6 in 1987 by
Methuen London Ltd
Copyright © 1987, 2000 by Deborah Levy
Clam first published in *Peace Plays* in 1985 by Methuen London Ltd
Copyright © 1985, 2000 by Deborah Levy
The B File first published in *Walks on Water* in 1992 by Methuen
Copyright © 1992 by Deborah Levy
Pushing the Prince into Denmark copyright © 2000 by Deborah Levy
Honey, Baby copyright © 2000 by Deborah Levy
Macbeth – False Memories copyright © 2000 by Deborah Levy
Collection and introduction copyright © 2000 by Deborah Levy

Deborah Levy has asserted her rights under the
Copyright, Designs and Patents Act 1988 to be identified
as the author of these works.

ISBN 0 413 75490 1

Methuen Publishing Limited Reg. No. 3543167

A CIP catalogue record for this book
is available from the British Library

Typeset by Deltatype Ltd, Birkenhead, Wirral
Printed and bound in Great Britain by
Cox & Wyman Ltd, Reading, Berks

Caution

Contents

Deborah Levy
A Chronology

1984   *Pax* directed by Lily Susan Todd (Women's Theatre Group)

1985   *Clam* directed by Anna Furse (Blood Group)
Ophelia and The Great Idea (stories)

1987   *Beautiful Mutants* (novel)
Heresies directed by Lily Susan Todd (RSC)

1990   *An Amorous Discourse In The Suburbs Of Hell* (poetry)

1991   *Pushing The Prince Into Denmark* – directed by Deborah Levy. RSC platform and Riverside Studios for Paines Plough Festival

1992   *Swallowing Geography* (novel)

1993   *Call Blue Jane* directed by Deborah Levy for *Man Act* Theatre, Chapter Arts, Cardiff; ICA, London; Royal Court Theatre, London
Editor of *Walks on Water* – Contemporary Performance Texts (Methuen)

1994   Libretto from Lorca's *Blood Wedding* – directed by Jules Wright, composed by Nicola Le Fanu, Rotherhithe Film Studios
Shiny Nylon, written and directed by Deborah Levy for The Women's Playhouse Trust, Royal Docks London
The Unloved (novel)

1995   *Honey, Baby*. Directed by Susanne Chaundry, LaMama, Melborne

1996   *Billy and Girl* (novel)

1997   'The Eros Of Rose'. Essay on the work of Rose English for *One Split Second of Paradise* (Rivers Oram)

1998   *Diary Of A Steak* (essay)

Preface

In my earliest twenties, I think I believed that theatre could change the world. Later, I discovered that my true interest in the theatre was that it was a place to connect with discomfort rather than prescriptions for how we might live. It took me a while to understand that when theatre uses all the languages that make it a unique form to write for (text, sound, design, lights, the spaces between actors, film and video), it is a place to make visual poetry, a place to show the human nervous system in a state of disquiet – in fact, to show some quite odd behaviour.

The early plays in this anthology, which I have titled 'Cold Wars', deal fairly surreally with aspects of the twentieth century – its holocausts and utopias and shattered dreams. It's strange now to think that I was so young, 23 years old, and felt so deeply about the very real possibility of nuclear war. I hope that future generations reading *Pax* and *Clam* will not have that same sense of urgency again.

Pushing the Prince into Denmark, *The B File* and *Honey, Baby* reflect my interest in turbulent, hybrid cultural and sexual identities. The theatre is an excellent place to explore how we (and particularly women) perform ourselves. Written in the 1990s, they echo much postmodern thinking, with its emphasis on fractured histories and geographies and its liberation from having to be authentic, whole and healed. This was very useful to me, as was theoretical writing that explored similar themes at the time by Julia Kristeva, Helene Cixous, Homi. K. Bhabha, Stuart Hall, Edward Said. I have rounded up these plays and pushed them under the sub-heading, 'Post-Modern Knots: Identity'.

Macbeth – False Memories, written in 2000, expresses a mood both in myself and I think more generally in the

UK – a feeling of being disconnected from any sense of shared values or ideological enthusiasms. I have subtitled this play, 'The Loss of God and Politics' because ultimately it is about a lack of feeling – a sort of millennial numbness, perhaps?

I should add that much of my work for the theatre has been both triumphed and trashed by critics. There has never been a calm assessment of what its value might be. I don't know whether this is a good or bad thing – only time will tell. As this anthology goes to press, I have just read an outraged review of *Macbeth – False Memories*; it says, 'Deborah Levy writes lines like "I haven't washed my pants since my father died." This disgust at death and female hygiene has compelled me to sit down and write a play called *Dirty Pants*,' which brings me to the last point I want to make in this introduction. I have come to realise that women laugh a great deal more than men – in life and in the theatre. I think all my new plays will be written with this in mind, because unlike my early twenties, when I was serious and scholarly and wanted to please, there is so much laughter inside me.

And I have always wanted the chignon worn at various times by both Simone de Beauvoir and Audrey Hepburn.

Deborah Levy
London, May 2000

1980s, Cold Wars

Introduction

When I received *Pax* I knew I was looking at something genuinely innovative. And I was a bit scared because it wasn't like anything I'd ever directed before. The play was made in a new language and I knew it was going to require all my art, in alliance with that of Anna Furse who had special skill in physical theatre, to create and sustain a concrete stage life for *Pax*. Gold had dropped into my hands! There were some sticky bits in the text, some incompleteness – it was, after all, a first full-length play from a young writer. Yet it was suffused with a mordant wit and a spirit of playful irony in a dramatic language that was alert, shapely, dynamic and very, very audacious. I was determined it should not be diluted or lose something of its startling individual voice when put through the mincer of a group critique. I knew I had to declare for *Pax* absolutely and planned what I would say when I met the cast for the first readthrough. 'We are so lucky to have this brilliant text to work on. We have a play we can trust in. We can begin rehearsal today.' *Pax* was one of the most critically acclaimed plays the Women's Theatre Group produced.

Lily Susan Todd
Director of the first production of *Pax*,
commissioned by the Women's Theatre Group.

Author's note

I was commissioned in 1984 by the Women's Theatre Group to write an 'anti-nuclear' play. I loathe those 'last two minutes in a bunker'-type scenarios so decided to write about twentieth-century Europe instead. Given such a large canvas I found four archetypes, who represented twentieth-century Europe for me.

The Keeper: I saw her as the past, and as Europe herself. A woman who carries the burden of history around with her.

The Hidden Daughter: I imagined as the future. Trying to make sense of the present. A young woman who trusts the evidence of her eyes and ears and is dismayed by that evidence.

The Mourner: The present. A woman who in Chekhov's words is in mourning for her own life. She is stuck and doesn't know how to move on.

The Domesticated Woman: She is both the present and the past. When I discovered her frailties, the bargains she has had to make to survive, I felt very fond of her.

Andrea Dworkin's astonishing book, *Right Wing Women* was a very useful source of insights.

Pax

Pax was first performed by the Women's Theatre Group at the Oval, London, on 20 August 1985, with the following cast:

Keeper	Eileen George
Mourner	Judy Elrington
Domesticated Woman	Christine Waterhouse
H.D.	Stephanie Pugsley

Directed by Lily Susan Todd with Anna Furse
Designed by Wendy Freeman
Music by Camilla Saunders
Stage Management Sue Baynton, Tierl Thompson
Lighting Design Veronica Wood
Administration Karin Gartzke, Jan Ryan

With special thanks to Lily Susan Todd, who nurtured the writing of *Pax* with her encouragement, inspiring intellect and glorious wit.

Characters

Keeper
Mourner
Domesticated Woman
H.D.

Setting

A large desolate house in the wilderness. It could be called 'The Retreat'.

Act One

Scene One: The Mourner's arrival

Night.

A very old statue of the Madonna and Child.
A buddha.
A vertical slab of marble.
Oil lamps / modern lamps.
A large globe of the world.
An oriental rug.
Wind chimes.
Some of these objects are covered with cloth. Emphasis on
Madonna and Child which is uncovered throughout.

Off, **Keeper**, *singing a lullaby. European accent.*

Keeper (*sings*)
    Hush little baba don't say a word
    Mama's going to buy you a mocking bird
    And if that mocking bird don't sing
    Mama's going to buy you a ruby ring
    And if that ruby ring goes brass
    Mama's going to buy you a looking-glass
    And if that looking-glass is cruel
    Mama's going to buy you a spinning wheel
    And if that spinning wheel don't spin . . .

A heavy old bell rings. **Keeper** *stops. Listens. Continues.*

    Mama's going to buy you a dog named Fritz
    And if that dog named Fritz don't bark
    Mama's going to bake you a honey cake
    And if that honey cake don't chew . . .

A modern piercing bell rings.

    Mama's going to buy you a bright blue shoe
    And if that bright blue shoe don't fit

You'll still be the best little baba in the world . . .

Both bells ring together, tentatively.

I want to go back to Prague.

Keeper *walks on. She wears a kimono tied at the waist with string; silver hair; diamanté earrings. She carries a lit candle; puts it down by the Madonna and Child. She holds up a heavy bunch of keys, sorting out which one she needs.*

Mourner *enters carrying a small, neat suitcase. Awkward, a little hunched.*
Keeper *is still sorting out keys.*

Mourner   I'm sorry. I didn't know which bell to ring.

Pause.

Sorry if I'm late.

Keeper   I was combing the dogs for wool.

Mourner   I got lost. There was no one about to get directions from.

Keeper   Come in!

Mourner   I am in.

Keeper *turns to look at her.*

Keeper   You look nothing like your mother.

Mourner   No.

Keeper   Your cheeks are red as Barcelona. Your mother was very pale.

Mourner   Not always.

She looks around the room.

Thank you for letting me come.

Keeper   Did you lose the map I sent you?

Mourner   No . . . I have it with me . . . I think you must have made a mistake. You sent me a map of Albania.

Keeper *laughs.*
Pause.

Keeper   Are you cold?

Mourner   A little. It was a long journey.

Keeper   Give me your hands.

Mourner *reluctantly does so.*
Keeper *looks at her palm as if doing a reading. She falls asleep still holding it. Wakes up.*

Keeper   Sit down.

She's at a loss. She jingles the wind chimes.

I will get you some schnapps and pretzels.

Mourner   Please don't go to any trouble.

Keeper   Everything is trouble.

She rummages about. She prepares a silver tray. She finds schnapps hidden in objects.

I bought a whole crate of this schnapps many years ago. From a Prussian spy. Prussian spies are always worth knowing because they don't get paid very well.

Pause.

You are subdued. It is to be expected.

Pause.

Mourner   I bought you a present. (*She opens her suitcase.*)

Keeper   Diamonds?

Mourner *hands a small plastic bag to* **Keeper**.

Keeper   Shells? (*She holds them to her ear.*)

Mourner   Fossils. I collected them on my last dig.

Keeper   HOW DARE YOU! How DARE you slip your insults into a plastic bag and pretend they're a gift!

Mourner   I'm sorry . . . I didn't mean to insult you . . . they're the remains of animals . . . preserved in the rocks . . . they're extremely rare . . .

Keeper *stamps on them.*

Mourner   Bones and tissue . . . *(She begins to cry.)* . . . they hold the shape of the original skeleton . . . delicate cell structures.

Keeper *stamps some more.*

Mourner   . . . I've preserved and classified them . . . it's my job . . . that one was perfectly symmetrical . . . they were very precious! *(She sobs.)*

Keeper *pours schnapps and gives some to* **Mourner** *who can't stop sobbing.*

Keeper   To your mother.

Mourner   Yes. Thank you.

She drinks and coughs and sobs some more.

I'm sorry. It takes me by surprise . . . since she died . . . it happened very suddenly . . . I wasn't prepared for it. I'm an archaeologist, you see . . . I didn't mean to be insulting . . .

Keeper   You wanted her to die on a fixed date? So you could preserve and classify her?

Mourner   No . . . I . . .

Keeper   WHY DID YOU COME HERE?

Mourner   I don't know . . . since she died . . . I've been very unhappy about everything . . . my job is to record the past . . . make sense of it . . . but *(She sobs.)* I

can't make sense out of anything any more . . . my
mother was a very secret woman . . . I thought you,
being her first cousin . . . might be able to help me . . .

Keeper I want to go back to Czechoslovakia.

Mourner My father left us when I was eleven. He
wasn't at the funeral.

Keeper She used to call him an ulcerous captain
of industry.

Mourner He was the managing director of an
electrical firm.

Keeper I know nothing about your mother.

She walks away, starts to light lamps.

Except that she played the piano with instinct and
originality. Did I hear her in Paris or Berlin? Or hell?
She created a language with her hands that was
unforgettable.

Mourner She was very proud of her hands. She wore
a copper bracelet to keep away rheumatism.

Keeper And then she stopped. The ulcerous captain
of industry did not have an ear for music I believe?

Mourner Towards the end of her life . . . she did
start to play again . . . but then she came out in a rash
. . . the itching was too much of a distraction.

Pause.

Keeper The dogs are howling in the yard. I refuse to
feed them.

Mourner There was no one . . . after she married . . .
she could . . . we were very different people . . . my
mother and I . . . she worked with abandon . . .
spontaneously . . . trying things out over and over
again . . .

Keeper *has fallen asleep on her feet.*

Mourner   I work with precision . . . reassembling fragments . . . everything is put into a plastic bag and labelled . . . excess and clutter distract me from detail . . . up to now there has always been a rational explanation for things . . .

Keeper (*wakes suddenly*)   Science can grapple with the irrational.

Mourner   And when she needed someone to talk to . . . (*She sobs.*) . . . I was too busy casting the skeleton of a small-boned hadrosaurus . . .

Keeper *takes a candle from the Madonna.*

Keeper   There is nothing as loving or as murderous as a mother's hand on her child.

Mourner *collects bits of broken fossil and puts them back in the plastic bag.*
Keeper *picks up* **Mourner**'s *suitcase.*

Keeper   Come. I'll take you to your room.

Mourner   I can carry that.

Keeper   I never had a suitcase. Only brown paper parcels. I wrapped everything in newspaper first.

Mourner   Please . . . let me . . .

Keeper   Sssssssh . . .

She leads **Mourner** *to her room. She hums the lullaby.*

It is not as comfortable as the Kaiserdorf Hotel. But it will do.

Mourner   Thank you very much.

Keeper   Hang out your clothes. Try to sleep.

Mourner   Yes.

Keeper *exits.*

Scene Two

Mourner *sits on the bed. After a while she finds hangers. She opens her suitcase and takes out a tape recorder. She starts to hang clothes.*

Keeper *unravels cloth to reveal a globe of the world. It lights up. She drinks schnapps, rolls globe in her hand.*

Keeper   My mother kept her darning in a Cartier box and said nothing. Obedience is not a virtue. My family were burnt in ovens.

Pause.

My father wore a square white beard and smelt of cologne. He was always crouched over the radio . . . or crouched over my mother. She smelt of cashew nuts.

She rolls the globe.

There I am. Young and full of hope. I wanted to choose to love. Not to be purchased for it. Lire. Francs. Roubles. Marks. And then . . . the women get pregnant . . . and nothing is certain any more. Men don't have to think about the relationship between their bodies and the next generation. They can deny their links with life . . .

She touches her earrings. She becomes very old.

Bribes? Or crocodile tears? Vhen I was twenty-one I achieved a heavy mink coat. Vell. If the mink is a persecuted animal . . . so am I.

Keeper *falls asleep.*
Mourner *plugs in the tape recorder. She speaks into it.*

Mourner   Seventy million years ago, at the close of the cretaceous, the earth was devastated. After its passing, there was no large animal left in existence. The few remaining birds, mammals, reptiles and land plants saw a drastic reduction in numbers. They inherited an earth that would have seemed empty.

Keeper   I want to go back to Yugoslavia.

Mourner   In the last few years of its dominion, the dinosaur was subjected to unbearable pressure. That much we know. (*Pause.*) That much I know. With their hormonal systems hopelessly out of balance, they left us a clue to the agony they must have suffered. (*Pause.*) The clue is in the eggs they left behind . . .

Piano starts to play. **Mourner** *stops.*

. . . A symptom of their stress . . . (*She listens.*) . . . the eggs started to get thinner and thinner . . . the embryo could not get enough calcium to build up its skeleton. That much I know. (*Pause.*) Those that did go through the ordeal of being laid . . . were born old . . . appearing from the shell with faces and bodies wrinkled with age. The fate of their offspring was sealed.

Mourner *switches off the tape recorder.*

H.D. (*offstage; whispers*)   I did know who I was when I got up this morning. Damn! Do I really belong to no one? I'm just going to have to smoke another cigar until I find out! Did I really see the sheep crop the grass this morning? Was it a cornfield or was it a missile base? My eyes are very bright and clear. That's one thing I do know. And my breathing is regular. Despite the cigars. To think I've never been kissed! Outrageous! Silly old woman! She doesn't even know what day it is. She says some cats have fur and some cats don't. I say it was either a cornfield or it was a missile base. Perhaps I'll understand all this when I grow up. But I *am* grown up! DAMN!

Scene Three

The sound of **Mourner** *sobbing in her sleep.*

Piano fading in and out, stopping and starting.

Mourner Mum?

Keeper (*stands over her bed with a candle*) No.

Mourner I can hear you.

Keeper No.

Mourner I can see your back bent over the piano . . .
I'm here . . . to the right of you . . . trying to catch your
eye . . . here to the left of you . . . trying to catch your
ear . . . here . . . under you . . . trying to touch your foot
as it presses the pedal . . .

Keeper So look at me.

Mourner *wakes, looks. Despair.*

Mourner (*sobs*) I *can* hear her.

Keeper Listen to me. I know what loss is. I have
been where you are now.

Pause.

I have been there. I have been to America . . . that
heartland of capitalism. I came back with a coronary
and a new nose. I have been to Russia. Twice. Once
when I witnessed the early optimism of communism, the
other when I witnessed old men leading us into the last
years of the twentieth century . . .

Mourner I want a biscuit . . .

Keeper I was there in 1918 when men murdered
their offspring and women were left to do the mourning.
I hired out crutches to the soldiers limping up to get
their medals and bought myself some hand cream . . .

Mourner   Tell me about her . . .

Keeper   I was there in Germany when they burnt knowledge. I knew when they burnt books they would burn people. I saw the pogroms in Romania and Czechoslovakia, Slavia, the Ukraine . . . plenty of bones for you to study there . . .

Mourner   I just wanted something nice to happen to her . . .

Keeper   I ate my fist in Monowitz and Belsen. And survived . . . just as you will survive . . .

Mourner   I can't pay my rent . . .

Keeper   I was there in Barcelona and Catalonia . . . when the world was a blister waiting to be pricked. The question? Who was going to prick it? And how do you heal a wound the size of the world? DO YOU KNOW WHAT SACRIFICE HUMAN BEINGS HAVE TO MAKE . . . IF THEY TRULY PUT THEIR SHOULDERS TO CHANGE . . . AND PUSH . . . JUST TO MOVE ONE INCH? I was there and wept hot tears when I saw another republic go down in blood.

Mourner   I've never done anything bad in my life . . .

Keeper   I was there in Nagasaki and Hiroshima. Saw human beings melt like plastic. When invading armies raped Manchuria, Ethiopia, China . . . I was there selling sandals and light bulbs . . .

Mourner   I just want a strawberry yoghurt . . .

Keeper   I counted the dead in Russia . . . twenty million . . . (*Pause.*) . . . my footprints are still in the snow. When the tanks crawled into Czechoslovakia and Hungary . . . I buried my Black Sea caviar in the garden . . . When America massacred hundreds and thousands of communists in Indo-China I dug it up again . . .

Mourner   I must get a grip on things . . .

Keeper   Felt the pulse of liberation in Cuba and Latin America . . . (*She holds her breath for a long time; exhales.*) . . . I know what unfinished business is . . . where you are now . . . you, the mourner, the grieving citizen of Europe . . . When they tried to reconstruct the desolate cities . . . I was there . . . a displaced person . . . like millions of others . . . looking for shelter and encouragement. I know the ghosts you think you see and hear . . . we are surrounded by ghosts . . . millions of our species slaughtered by our own hand . . . (*She yawns.*) . . . we cannot redeem ourselves . . . we can only free . . . ourselves . . . (*She falls asleep.*)

H.D. (*sings*)
Who's to say
what's right
or wrong
when i don't even know
who i am
perhaps i am
a bicycle
perhaps i am
la la la la

I like rabbits
and cigars
swimming in the lake
i like to know
about history
so I can learn
about me
perhaps i won't
perhaps i will
la la la.

Blackout.

Scene Four: The Domesticated Woman's arrival

Morning.

The table laid for breakfast.
Mourner *and* **Keeper** *are seated at the table. Both tap boiled eggs in unison.* **Mourner** *stops.* **Keeper** *taps.* **Mourner** *and* **Keeper** *tap in unison.* **Keeper** *eats.* **Mourner** *taps. Stops.*

Keeper   I remember breakfasting with Freud and Salvado Dali . . . a small but stylish café in Vienna. Dali wrapped his penis in an omelette.

Mourner *smiles wanly. She taps her egg.*

Keeper   Freud applauded. (*She eats.*) Very loudly if I remember. 'All this man vants to do,' he said, 'is crawl back into the egg. LOOK . . . ve vitness it now!'

She walks to the buddha. She produces egg from behind his ear.

Sigmund asked me what I thought of his theories . . .

Mourner   What did you say?

Keeper   I told him to stop stealing my eggs! Churchill was partial to eggs. We ate together at the Ritz. He dribbled yolk all over his bow tie. Mind you, he was fairly preoccupied at the time . . . (*She impersonates badly.*) . . . 'If we don't put our foots on the egg we will have to chase the chickens round the farmyards of the worlds!' He was talking about the Bolsheviks of course! By the time we finished breakfast he had egg all over his chins!

Mourner   When I woke up this morning I smelt cigar smoke.

Keeper   Really? He hasn't stayed here for years.

Keeper *gets up. She uncovers the marble vertical slab and polishes with her sleeve.*

Mourner   It felt as if someone had been standing over me – watching me. My clothes had been touched and my tape recorder tampered with.

Keeper   You think it's Goldilocks?

Mourner   It frightens me.

Keeper (*polishing hard*)   It's normal to be frightened. A slab of the Third Reich. Untouched by the blemish of need and disorder. (*She spits at the slab.*) When I was twenty-six my back was covered in boils.

Mourner   I was too scared to open my eyes.

Keeper (*rage*)   EAT YOUR EGG!

The old bell rings.
Pause.
Mourner *cracks the eggshell.*

Mourner   I don't know what I'll find inside it.

The new bell rings.

Keeper   I want to go back to Romania.

Keeper *takes out her bunch of keys. She tries to sort out which one she needs.*
Both bells ring.
Pause.

Domesticated Woman *enters. She carries a blooming cactus plant. She has bleached, styled hair and bright modern clothes.*

Domesticated Woman   Well, hello! Sorry. I didn't know which bell to ring.

Pause.

I got terribly lost. There wasn't a soul about to get directions from!

Keeper   I was combing the dogs for wool. Come in.

Domesticated Woman   I am in.

Keeper *turns to look at her. They stare for a long time.*

Domesticated Woman   It's been a long time.

Keeper   Did you lose the map I sent you?

Domesticated Woman   I think you must have made a mistake. You sent me a map of Moscow.

Keeper *laughs.*

Keeper   Your lips are blue as Iran. Are you cold?

Domesticated Woman   A little. It was a long journey. (*She looks around her.*)

Keeper   I prefer hotels. For their warmth, luxury and complete lack of household responsibilities.

Domesticated Woman   I sympathise with you. (*She sees* **Mourner**.) Well, hello!

Mourner (*small voice*)   Hello.

Domesticated Woman   You must be . . .

Keeper (*quick*)   Your niece.

Domesticated Woman   Poor little thing. (*She kisses her tenderly.*) Let me look at you. The spitting image of your mother. Isn't she?

Pause.

Domesticated Woman *strokes* **Mourner**'*s hair.*

Domesticated Woman   I've been thinking about you.

Keeper   The dogs are howling in the yard. They have not been fed this morning.

She exits.

Domesticated Woman (*takes* **Mourner**'*s hands*)   I'm your mother's big sister. And you're her daughter.

(*Pause.*) I feel a little tearful. (*She laughs.*) Did she ever talk to you about me?

Mourner   No.

Domesticated Woman   Well, we didn't always see eye to eye ... but life's like that. I'm sorry things turned out for her like they did ... I really am. But now I've met you! And we've got all the time in the world to find out about each other.

Mourner   When did you last see her?

Domesticated Woman   Not since your father left. (*Brisk.*) I have a very busy life of my own back home. Three beautiful sons to take care of. I bought this plant at the airport to remind me of them – look – it's got three blooms exactly ... this one here is Scott ... he's the eldest and most sensitive ... he's a policeman ... and this firm bloom here ... is Brem ... he's a farmer ... and this young bud ... the baby of them all is my youngest – Mark – he's stationed not too far from here – somewhere near a cornfield. I try not to think about how much I miss him.

Keeper *returns.*

Keeper   Would you like an egg and pretzels?

Domesticated Woman   I'd love the egg. Don't know about the pretzels. But I do have a roll. I saved it from the plane. There. Help yourself. (*She takes a roll and gives it to* **Mourner**.)

Mourner   Thank you!

Domesticated Woman   Do you have a little slab of butter?

Keeper   What is butter but a poor milked cow like myself?

She takes an enormous egg from the buddha and gives it to the
Domesticated Woman.

Eagle. Bird of prey.

Pause.

Mourner   Where did you find it?

Keeper   Under my armpit.

Domesticated Woman (*smiles*)   Thank you. (*To*
Mourner.) You haven't eaten a thing. I know your
appetite probably isn't what it should be . . . so soon
after . . . but try and eat a little.

Mourner   I don't eat eggs.

Keeper (*rage*)   WELL WHY DIDN'T YOU SAY?

Domesticated Woman *taps her egg.*
Pause.

Domesticated Woman (*to* **Keeper**)   I bought you
a present. (*She hands her a package.*)

Keeper   Pumpkin cake? Pecan pie?

She unwraps the present, bewildered.

What is it? (*She waves it in the air.*)

Domesticated Woman   An electric carving knife.
Saves time and saves waste. I have one at home. Just
like that.

Keeper (*waving the knife like a cutlass*)   HOW DARE
YOU! HOW DARE YOU INSULT ME! YOU KNOW
I DON'T EAT MEAT! (*She tries to bend the knife.*)

Domesticated Woman   I didn't mean to insult you. I
had no idea you don't eat meat. Perhaps you can find
another use for it? (*To* **Mourner**.) I want you to know
that you always have a home with us . . . (**Keeper**
laughs.) . . . and your uncle just loves meeting pretty girls.

She taps her egg apprehensively.

I get terrible headaches. (*She rummages around.*)

Keeper I want to go back to Slavia and eat schnitzel.

Mourner I thought you said you didn't eat meat.

Domesticated Woman She's allowed to change her mind, isn't she? I can't find my headache pills, but I have found a letter from Mark – I'm sure he'd love to meet you!

Keeper *laughs.*

Domesticated Woman Are you sure this egg is sound?

Keeper No.

Domesticated Woman (*whispers to* **Mourner**) Do you think she's trying to poison me?

Keeper Yes.

Domesticated Woman I thought you might have mellowed with age.

Keeper I'm not a vat of wine.

Domesticated Woman You're certainly full of sour grapes!

Keeper Halfvit!

Mourner If you don't want that egg . . . do you think I could have it?

Domesticated Woman Sure. Are you that hungry?

Mourner I'm interested in eggs.

Domesticated Woman Uh-huh. (*She stares at her.*)

Pause.

Mourner Did my mother want to have me?

Domesticated Woman   Well, I'm sure she was very happy when you arrived. Children make a woman feel valuable. We all have to make sacrifices in this world . . . because children are an investment for the future . . . and a special gesture of love between the husband and wife making it! Your womb is your wealth!

Keeper   Patriots invent electric chairs.

Domesticated Woman (*to* **Mourner**)   And you've got to cheer up! I try to smile even when I'm feeling miserable.

H.D. (*offstage; loudly*)   SILLY OLD WOMAN! I'M GOING TO SMOKE ALL YOUR BLACK-MARKET CIGARS AND READ ALL YOUR DIARIES!!

Pause.

Mourner   Who was that?

Domesticated Woman   Sorry?

Mourner   A girl . . .

Keeper   The dogs . . .

Mourner   A girl . . . she said . . . what did she say?

Pause.

Domesticated Woman (to the **Mourner**)   Why don't we go for a walk? Talk the air and pick some pretty flowers for the table?

Mourner   I keep hearing voices . . . all through the night . . .

Domesticated Woman (*takes her hand*)   Your mother was scared of the dark too.

Mourner   I get cramps in my legs . . . (*She starts to sob.*)

Keeper   I HAFF HAD ENOUGH SNOT AND TEARS FOR ONE MORNING!

Mourner   Sorry. (*She sobs.*)

Domesticated Woman   You know, when you've been bereaved . . . and you're not feeling as strong as you should do . . . it's quite common to hear voices and have hallucinations . . . it takes a while to get your body back to normal again . . . you must try not to be too impatient, sweetheart . . .

Mourner   I've got to get back to work . . . get my life back together again . . .

Keeper   YA. Good idea. Fuck off.

Mourner   . . . Clean the windows . . . empty the bins . . . feed the tortoise . . . (*She sobs.*) . . . I don't know what there is to look forward to any more . . .

Domesticated Woman   I sympathise with you . . .

Mourner   I'm an archaeologist . . . I have to dig . . . excavate . . . now I'm too frightened to even pick up the spade . . .

Domesticated Woman   You need someone to take care of you that's all. Why don't you go and put on something warm and we'll take the air.

Keeper   I will NOT have my air breathed.

Mourner (*gets up; to* **Keeper**)   Sorry. (*She exits.*)

Keeper   Why have you come to disturb my repose?

Domesticated Woman   Why are you so harsh with me all the time and with everyone else too?

Mourner *enters. She takes the large egg. She exits.*

Domesticated Woman   You don't understand human nature at all do you? (*Pause.*) I also have memories that refuse to go away. I wanted to see what she looks like, what kind of human being she's grown up into. It's only natural . . .

Keeper   Nothing is natural.

Domesticated Woman   Don't get me wrong. I am really very happy. I have a bright clean house . . . warm towels every day . . . a refrigerator stuffed with goodies . . . a garden full of beautiful sunflowers . . .

Keeper   I have nothing to say to you.

Domesticated Woman   I have plenty to say and it's not to you.

Mourner *enters wearing a thick coat.*

Mourner   I'm ready.

Domesticated Woman   Good. I need to stretch my legs after the journey. And we've got so much to talk about.

Domesticated Woman *and* **Mourner** *go out.*
Keeper *walks to the table, picks up one of the eggshells and smashes it.*

Keeper   One beautiful daughter!

H.D. (*offstage*)   A quiver, a bow, a cauldron, a spindle, a spoon, a mirror, a wreath of string . . . bringing the soul's travel back to its place of origin. I want to know where I originated. I want to know who I am. And I won't bath every day. I won't!

Keeper (*sings*)
War came to me one day
Sucked all the colour
From my eye
I said, hold on,
I need that
For the Revolution
But War just sucked away

H.D. (*offstage*)   I know I saw the priests bless the bombs . . . in the cornfield. But they were wearing suits and

carried briefcases. OH SOMETIMES I FEEL LIKE
THROWING MYSELF UNDER A HORSE! Who was
my father?

Keeper (*sings*)
   Border after border
   I crossed
   until my fate
   came out right
   But when it came to defending myself
   My hands were too tired
   to fight
   And War just sucked away.

Wind chimes.
Blackout.

Scene Five

Night.

Domesticated Woman *in front of a mirror. She puts on
face cream.*
Mourner *is in her 'room'.*
Keeper *is asleep.*

Domesticated Woman   I am totally beautiful to my
husband. Whether I'm making salad, making love,
playing tennis, or even having a good cry. There's so
much . . . ugliness around us.

Mourner (*into her tape recorder*)   Dinosaurs were the
moderns . . . they were constantly moving forward . . . in
order to walk faster and more efficiently they went up
on two legs instead of four. The archaic tortoise and
turtle kept their slow sprawling walk. They are still with
us today. In all fairness it should have been their lot to
disappear . . .

Piano music creeps in.

But then . . . those that had flourished the most . . .
suffered the greatest losses . . . (*Pause.*) . . . The small
inherited the earth . . .

Piano gets louder.

. . . The small inherited the earth. (*She switches off the tape.*)

H.D. (*offstage*)   Today on my walk I saw that the leaves
and trees were covered in a sticky substance. I know the
trees very well. The substance was like heavy oil . . .
except colourless. I think it's nerve gas . . . (*She sighs.*)

Ripple of sighs from everyone.

Shall I poison myself with sloe gin? (*Pause.*) No. I will
have to build up my antibodies. But first I must put a
cross on my wall and mark this day. Where's my pen?
DAMN!! Nothing is in its right place.

Keeper   The dogs are sick. They have not touched
their food.

Scene Six

Piano music.

Mourner *sobbing in her sleep.* **Domesticated Woman**
stands over her with face cream on. She shakes her shoulder gently.

Domesticated Woman   Sssshh. Sssshh . . .

Mourner *wakes and screams at the white-faced* **Domesticated
Woman**

Domesticated Woman   Sssshh. It's only me . . . I'm
your aunt . . .

Mourner *recovers from her convulsive sobs.*
Domesticated Woman *sits on* **Mourner**'s *bed and hugs
her.*

Mourner He threw her music into the fire . . . she tried to rescue it and burnt her hands . . .

Domesticated Woman Would you like an aspirin?

Mourner *shakes her head.*

Domesticated Woman It's difficult for a man. To love a woman who sleeps with a pen and paper under her pillow and rushes out of bed in the middle of the night to play the piano . . . and it's difficult for a child too – when you want her attention and she's giving it all to something else.

Piano gets louder.

Mourner I dreamt she was murdered.

Keeper *laughs.*

Mourner I liked the sound of her playing at night. It comforted me . . . (*She sobs.*) . . . I just don't like the sound of her playing now she's dead.

Domesticated Woman I bet she was too tired in the mornings to make breakfast!

Mourner If she hadn't had me to care for . . .

Domesticated Woman We mustn't fight nature. We must celebrate it. Not deny it. It's the most precious thing we've got and one day you'll have beautiful children. It's your destiny.

Mourner It wasn't my mother's destiny.

Domesticated Woman (*after a pause*) I am the land and my husband is the farmer.

Mourner She used to feed me turnip water for the vitamin C . . .

Domesticated Woman   I think Ribena would have tasted a lot nicer, don't you?

Piano fades out.

Mourner (*laughs*)   Yes. (*They both laugh.*)

Domesticated Woman   That's better! See! It's stopped!

Mourner   So you heard it too.

Domesticated Woman   The rain. It's stopped at last. Look what I've got! Chocolate! I always save some for the nights when I can't sleep . . . or when I'm thinking things I shouldn't be thinking . . .

Mourner   Thank you.

Both eat chocolates.

Domesticated Woman   You're a very intelligent woman.

Mourner *shakes her head.*

Domesticated Woman   Oh you are. The thing is . . . intelligence makes a woman unhappy.

Mourner   I'm recording everything. I've even written my name and date of birth on the wall of my bedsit.

Domesticated Woman   You should use your intelligence to find yourself a smart husband. (*She gives her more chocolate.*)

Mourner   Do you think that would make me any happier?

Domesticated Woman   As long as you hide away a few treats for yourself.

Domesticated Woman *eats more chocolate. Feels her face. Thinks.*

Scene Seven

Night.

H.D. *enters carrying a fishing rod and a bucket, smoking a cigar.*

H.D. Not even a small trout! DAMN! I'm going to have to make another rod, cast more nets. Study the tides. But if the fish are dead there's not much point!

Pause.

Cod, winkles, shellfish! On their backs. And the plants are eating themselves. The only thing there's plenty of is rats!

Domesticated Woman *turns round and sees* **H.D.***; they stare at each other.*

Domesticated Woman I wondered when I was going to meet you!

H.D. Did *you* poison the fish?

Domesticated Woman Why, I don't think so. Do you often go fishing at this time of night? (**H.D.** *nods.*) Now wouldn't it be a whole lot easier to do it in daylight?

H.D. A dead fish is a dead fish.

Domesticated Woman I suppose it is.

Pause.

H.D. Did you put sticky oil on the plants and leaves?

Domesticated Woman Sticky oil?

H.D. Why do you keep a gun under your pillow?

Domesticated Woman Why, I'm beginning to feel as if I'm in a court room. (*Pause.*) Do you know who I am?

H.D.   I know nothing except the fish are dead!

Domesticated Woman   Do you really know nothing?

H.D.   KNOWING ALL THE FISH ARE DEAD IS QUITE A BIG THING TO KNOW!

Domesticated Woman   You have a temper just like your father!

H.D. (*quiet*)   Who was my father?

Domesticated Woman   Come – let me kiss you.

H.D. (*shy*)   I've . . . never been kissed before. WELL IT'S OUTRAGEOUS THAT I'VE NEVER BEEN KISSED!

Domesticated Woman   Surely your mother kisses you?

H.D.   Never!

Domesticated Woman *walks over to* **H.D.** *and pecks her on the cheek.*

H.D.   Oh. (*Pause.*)

She kisses **Domesticated Woman** *then holds her face out to be kissed again.* **Domesticated Woman** *kisses her.*

Oh.

She kisses **Domesticated Woman** *again and then holds out her cheek again.* **Domesticated Woman** *kisses her once more.*

Oh. (*Pause.*) Is my father still alive?

Domesticated Woman   Do you go to school?

H.D.   I play the piano.

Domesticated Woman   Ah. I thought it was you.

H.D.   Is he?

Domesticated Woman   Do you really know nothing at all?

H.D.   Are you trying to make me feel like a sardine? Are you? Can sardines kiss? All I know is that I'm inventing a spinning wheel. And when it's finished I'm going to make the silly old woman a shawl. She's collecting hair from the dogs.

Domesticated Woman   Well, isn't that nice? If I'd known you were interested in crafts I would have bought you a wheel. You would have to put the parts together yourself – but the instructions are in the box.

H.D.   Has one already been made?

Domesticated Woman   Funny little girl! It was invented centuries ago.

H.D.   Who was my father? Well? Tell me ma'am, sir . . . and why is your son at the missile base?

Domesticated Woman   I don't know what you're talking about.

H.D.   IT'S ALL RIGHT! I'm in a bad mood. Because the plants are eating themselves. (*She paces around.*) *SHE* knows . . . (*She points in the direction of* **Mourner**'s *room.*)

Domesticated Woman   Who?

Mourner   The mourner. She knows. I like her. And her dinosaurs.

Domesticated Woman   Dinosaurs?

H.D.   I listened to her tape. She's got a dead mother.

Domesticated Woman   I could have been your mother.

H.D.   Oh.
IS MY FATHER STILL ALIVE?

Domesticated Woman (*sentimental*)   No sweetheart.
I'm afraid he's not.

H.D.   Well, there's no need to look sad. Or make
a sad voice. Or make a sad kiss for me. (*Pause.*) Was he
a good man?
DAMN! They always go out when I need them! (*She
throws away her cigar.*)

Domesticated Woman   And very bad for your lungs
too. Your father wouldn't have approved.

H.D.   Oh?

Domesticated Woman   I mean medically . . . not
morally . . . he was a doctor, you see.

H.D.   A DOCTOR! A DOCTOR! I'm so proud! (*She
embraces* **Domesticated Woman**.) HE MADE PEOPLE
HEALTHY!

Domesticated Woman   Sssshh! I'm glad I came.
You've made me very happy. I wanted to see you.
You particularly.

H.D.   And you're going to tell me everything!

Domesticated Woman   I'd like to!

H.D.   And you're not going to tell me any lies!

H.D. *kisses her and fingers her dress and hair.*

Domesticated Woman   I never tell lies.

H.D.   And you're such a strange fish . . . your smell
. . . chocolate . . . face paint . . . aspirins . . . tissues . . .
your hair . . . (*She touches her hair again.*)

Domesticated Woman   Mind! Stop it!

As **H.D.** *strokes* **Domesticated Woman**'s *hair a wig
comes off in her hand.*

Give it back!

H.D., *astonished, looks at the wig. She puts it in her bucket.*

H.D.   But you promised you wouldn't tell lies!

Blackout.

Act Two

Scene One

Day.

Domesticated Woman *watering her plant, singing.*

Domesticated Woman (*sings*)
Love me tender
Love me trooooooooe
Never let me go
For my darling I love you
And I always will
Love me tender
Love me trooooooooe . . .

Keeper *enters.*

Domesticated Woman I polished all the shoes in the hall . . .

Keeper Hmmm.

Domesticated Woman And I've cleaned the kitchen cupboards . . .

Keeper Hmmmm . . .

Domesticated Woman And I scrubbed the bath. It was full of seaweed . . . And I met your daughter.

Keeper *looks distraught. She rattles the wind chimes.*
Mourner *enters.*

Mourner I've weeded your garden.

Keeper Hmmm.

Mourner And glued the broken tiles in your study . . . And picked holes in the soles of my feet and couldn't stop.

Keeper   Hmmmmm ...

Mourner   And tried to drown myself in the river.

Keeper   Hmmmm ...

Mourner   And watched the peacocks strutting about the yard. They make such a terrible sound in their throats.

Domesticated Woman   That means they're courting. And you and me are going to make apple pie tonight for EVERYONE's supper.

Keeper   H.D.! I TAKE IT WITH ICE AND MINT TODAY!

Pause.

Domesticated Woman (*back at her plant*)
   Love me tender ...
   Love me trooo ...

Keeper (*angry*)   H.D.! ICE IT AND MINT IT AND BRING IT IN!

Domesticated Woman
   Never let me go ...

The sound of footsteps. **H.D.** *peers through the curtains.*

H.D.   You take it with cinnamon today.

Keeper (*raging*)   So why don't I make a small revolution and have it with mint? WILL THE WORLD BLOW UP IF I HAVE IT WITH MINT?

H.D. *disappears.*

Keeper   WILL YOUR CIGAR SHRIVEL IF I HAVE IT WITH MINT?
WILL YOUR EARS DROP OFF IF I HAVE IT WITH MINT?
WILL ANGELS HAVE ORGIES IF I HAVE IT WITH MINT?

H.D. *comes on with a cup of mint tea and a hair brush.*

Keeper (*to* **Mourner**)   This is my daughter. Her name is H.D. H.D., this woman is a very distant cousin of sorts – she collects fossils and picks holes in the soles of her feet.

H.D. *walks up to* **Mourner**, *compares their heights and stares.*

H.D. (*puffing on her cigar*)   I saw you watching the peacocks. Why did you take those feathers?

Keeper   HAFF YOU BEEN PLUCKING MY PEACOCKS? HAFF YOU? MY BEAUTIFUL IMPORTED PEACOCKS? HAFF YOU BEEN PUTTING MY PLUMAGE INTO A PLASTIC BAG? HAFF YOU?

Mourner (*begins to sob*)   I . . . just . . .

Domesticated Woman   Don't cry – she's in a bad mood today. That's all.

Keeper   I HAVE NO SUCH THING AS BAD MOODS!

Domesticated Woman *gives* **Mourner** *a tissue.*

Keeper   I do not like to be blackmailed. I haff had enough of it. And it has always been from imbeciles such as yourself who haff nothing to do with their life but invest in other people's distress. H.D. – I believe you haff met this woman?

H.D.   Yes. She taught me how to kiss.

Keeper (*stomps across the stage and rattles the wind chimes; to* **Domesticated Woman**)   From now on I call you Maligma. That is your name M-A-L-I-G-M-A, MALIGMA. I haff never loved Americans.

Domesticated Woman   If you want to indulge your

personal prejudices . . .

H.D.   I've never been in a room with so many people before. Is this how people behave? When they're together? (*To* **Mourner**.) Is it?

Mourner   I don't know.

H.D.   I heard your tape. I played it when you were outside. Most interesting. That it is! Would you like a cigar? (**Mourner** *doesn't answer.*) Oh. (*Pause.*) What do you think about bees? (**Mourner** *doesn't answer. Pause.*) What are you going to do with your findings?

Mourner   Throw them in the river.

Domesticated Woman   She's not feeling very well today.

Mourner   I want to know exactly *why* the earth was devastated . . . and why dinosaurs . . . after one hundred and fifty million years . . . suddenly died off . . .

H.D.   Yes. I want to know too.

Mourner   One theory is that the plants waged chemical warfare . . .

Domesticated Woman   Nonsense! You're both talking nonsense.

Mourner   Dinosaurs had huge appetites and ate the plants in vast quantities. To protect themselves the plants made themselves poisonous . . . the tortoise and turtle survived because they ate much less.

Domesticated Woman   What a lot to worry about! We should start peeling apples soon. And now we've got an extra guest!

Keeper   H.D. IS NOT A GUEST! *YOU* ARE A GUEST!

H.D. (*to* **Keeper**)   I'll do your hair.

Keeper   Ah – COIFFURE!

H.D. *brushes* **Keeper**'s *hair.*

Keeper   Oh, I do love to have my hair brushed. H.D., your hands are gentle as clouds in spring. I do love to feel your warm breath on my neck.

H.D.   You have such beautiful silver hair. Perhaps I will too when I grow up. BUT I AM GROWN UP! DAMN!

Keeper   Oh, don't shout . . .

H.D. (*shouting to* **Domesticated Woman**)   Hasn't she got lovely hair?

Domesticated Woman (*to* **Mourner**)   Shall we go and peel the apples?

Keeper   Goot idea. A little to the left H.D. Go and bake us all a pie. And please . . . dress for dinner. And you (*To* **Mourner**.) . . . come here . . . feel free to decorate yourself with peacock feathers . . . and H.D. . . . when you have finished my hair . . . I must feed the dogs . . .

H.D.   The dogs are dead.

Keeper   DEAD?

H.D.   Cancer.

Sound of high-pitched whine.

Scene Two

Before dinner.

Mourner *is peeling a large apple.*

Mourner   If I can peel the skin off in one complete circle . . . without breaking . . . it will make the shape of

the first letter of my lover's name.
That's what she said.
I can also make a wish.
I don't know what to wish and anyway I don't have
a lover.
Anyway . . . it looks like a wreath.
Did she only die two hours ago? Or was it a month?
I think I'm going to die. Everything is marked for death.
And there's a worm in this apple.
I should be using my hands to restore the great tusked
tortoise. Or the toad with the stumpy tail. It was my
idea to put them on display. Now I don't have ideas
about anything any more.

A loud rabbit squeal.

Domesticated Woman *(offstage)*   GOTCHA!

Scene Three

Night.

The table is laid for supper. **Domesticated Woman**,
H.D., **Mourner** *all stand round the table. All are dressed for
dinner.* **Mourner** *wears a peacock feather.* **Domesticated
Woman** *wears oven gloves and holds a huge porcelain dish.
Rustling offstage.*
Keeper *appears dressed as Elizabeth I and stands dramatically.*

Keeper   Although I have the weak and feeble body of
a man, I have the heart and stomach of a woman! SIT!

All sit.

STAND!

All stand.

There is something we have forgotten to do. Would the
mourner please pass me her feather.

H.D.   You said she could wear it.

Mourner *takes off the feather. She hands it to* **Keeper** *who waves it in the air.*

Keeper   Caressing the void! SIT!

All sit. **Keeper** *puts the feather back on* **Mourner**.

Domesticated Woman   Fig leaves in pistachio sauce! (*She holds the porcelain dish up in the air then serves out the food in it.*)

Keeper (*holds up a decanter of red wine*)   A present from a small collective in Normandy! (*She pours wine.*)

H.D.   What *is* inside the fig leaves?

Domesticated Woman   Lots of goodies. Just eat up.

H.D.   What did you put inside them?

Mourner   Rabbit.

H.D. (*screams*)   OH NO! They killed the black rabbit!

Keeper   Don't be so sentimental – when half the world cannot eat!

Domesticated Woman   You can't fill your belly with tobacco.

H.D. (*sobs*)   Not the black rabbit!!

Domesticated Woman   There are plenty more rabbits hopping about all over the place.

H.D.   I WILL NOT EAT RABBIT.

Domesticated Woman (*spooning her own portion*)   Well, that's some gratitude, isn't it? And after we've been working so hard to make this a jolly evening.

H.D.   Did you break its neck?

Pause.

Mourner The electric carving knife.

H.D. *sobs noisily.*

Keeper Oh my innocent daughter. (*She lifts her glass.*)
May all who harvest drink. (*She swigs wine.*)

Domesticated Woman Shall we say grace?

Keeper But of course. H.D. and I will pray. When in
Rome do as the Greeks do. H.D.!

H.D. You never get it right anyway.

Keeper My pagan daughter. YOU WILL PRAY!

H.D. *and* **Keeper** *put their hands together, shut their eyes, sing
the notes of the piano scale.*

Keeper
H.D. } *La la la la la la la la . . .*

Mourner *and* **Domesticated Woman** *look at each other.*

All La la la la la la la la.

Mourner *gets stuck on the last note and drones for a very long
time. It becomes a kind of primitive wailing.*
H.D. *and* **Keeper** *start their meal.* **H.D.** *picks at her food.*
Domesticated Woman *nudges* **Mourner**'s *shoulder.*

Domesticated Woman I think we've finished
now . . .

H.D. I will only eat the sauce.

Keeper I would smile except all my teeth are rotten.

H.D. Poor rabbit.

Mourner *finishes wailing. She sits down.*

Mourner I'm broken . . .

The others continue to eat.

I'm going to meet her on the bridge . . . and give her

the teapot I glued together. The one I smashed. She'll be wearing her green coat.

Domesticated Woman   She needs to see a doctor.

H.D.   My father was a doctor!

Keeper   EAT YOUR RABBIT!

Domesticated Woman (*holds up her glass*)   Cheers! To all of us! And to happier times. (*To* **Mourner**.) Time does heal, you know.

H.D. (*to* **Keeper**)   MY FATHER WAS A DOCTOR AND YOU NEVER TOLD ME!

Keeper   I want to go back to Essex . . .

H.D. (*points at* **Domesticated Woman**)   She knew my father! She said she could nearly have been my mother! How can I dive into the river if I don't know what I'm diving into? All the fish are dead! And I don't know why . . .

Keeper (*holds up her glass*)   A hint of sediment . . .

H.D.   I don't know what I'm drinking.

Keeper   What I really want . . . crave for . . . would give my ruff for . . . is pumpernickel . . .

Domesticated Woman   That's why you're putting on weight. It's all you used to eat in those days too . . .

Keeper   And you ate artichokes and hothouse lettuces . . .

H.D.   So did my rabbit!

Keeper   And steak and *swein* and French chocolates and Japanese rice cakes, made available to you for a mere kiss . . .

Mourner   When I'm reassembling bones I think of her bones . . . her heart . . . lungs . . . pelvis . . . and I have to stop . . .

Domesticated Woman (*pats* **Mourner** *on the back*) Swallow what's in your mouth first . . .

H.D. Bring it all up – every bit of gristle.

Domesticated Woman I can tell she's not used to eating with people.

H.D. I'm not used to eating my pets!

Mourner And I have to stop . . . and then I can't do overtime any more . . . and then I can't pay my rent . . .

Keeper I want to go back . . .

H.D. SILLY OLD WOMAN!

Domesticated Woman I have never pretended that I don't like the good things in life. And why shouldn't I? Why shouldn't we be healthy and happy and like nice things? What a horrible world you want for us all. Well, come on, girls . . . H.D. – you've got a sweet young voice – sing for us!

H.D. (*sings*)
    I had a rabbit
    Her eyes were pink
    Her name was Antigone
    She drove me to drink
    But I *loved* her
    Loved her . . .

Mourner Where are my tools? If I can't find my tools I can't work . . . and if I can't work I can't shop at Sainsbury's . . . (*She stuffs food in her mouth.*) . . . I don't know where to begin . . .

Keeper Tell me, Maligma . . . (*She pours* **Domesticated Woman** *more wine.*) . . . why did you give up chemistry? Vas that not vhat you were studying in Berlin . . . vhen I vas stuffing myself with

pumpernickel? . . . do I not recall seeing you with books
tucked under your arm . . . fingers stained with acid . . .
hair curled with litmus paper? Do I not recall you
studying for exams . . . watching your Sviss watch with
its seventy-nine jewels . . . in the bar of the Kaiserdorf
Hotel where I sat opposite you . . . observing your
young body ooze small clues to your admirer? . . . did
I not watch all this . . . dressed as a nun . . . yellow star
stitched to my heart? . . . and do I not recall H.D.'s
father driving you home in an elegant voisine . . . black
as a hearse? and did he not undress you *à la chambre* . . .
and did you not reveal elegant silk lingerie . . . black as
a hearse? Yes rabbit and pistachio is very goot . . . very
goot . . . it loosens the tongues does it not . . .
pumpernickel loosens the bowels . . . So tell me about
your studies . . . your passions . . . and your distractions
. . . and were your dreams as black as your licorice
bonbons . . . kittens . . . seamed stockings . . . jet
bracelets . . . and your heart?

Domesticated Woman (*to* **Mourner**)　Ha ha. How
are you doing, Honey?

Keeper　NO! What are you doing? Have you given
that some thought?

H.D.　I can't bear it. I just can't bear it!

Keeper　Vell, you are going to haff to bear it.

Domesticated Woman　I've made ice cream
for pudding.

Mourner　If I can't pay my rent I won't have
anywhere to live. I never had anyone to support me . . .

H.D.　WHO WAS MY FATHER?

Mourner　WHO WAS MY MOTHER?

Keeper　Who vas Rosie Finklestein?

H.D.   Answer me, you stupid old woman. All your teeth are rotting and your toenails fall off in the bath.

Keeper   Ask Maligma. I have never been one to pay off my debts. And if I had you would have ended up in the poor house. Or even worse . . . AMERICA!

Domesticated Woman   You didn't love him.

Keeper   Correct.

H.D.   Who? Who didn't you love?

Domesticated Woman   Your father, sweetie. She doesn't know how to love anything. And she makes people who do look stupid.

Keeper   Love does not come into this equation. The word is redundant.

Domesticated Woman   Oh, it's not. It's not.

Mourner   My periods have stopped.

Keeper   So haff mine.

H.D.   Why didn't you love him?

Keeper   I have never been partial to fair-skinned men.

Domesticated Woman   You took bribes to save your skin.

Keeper   And you bribe your way through the week with smiles and chocolate cookies.

Pause.

Your father shot my kitten. She was called Vera Vaslova.

Domesticated Woman   What's wrong with a proper name like Snowy?

H.D.   Why did you make love with him then? Why did you let him touch your silver hair?

Silence.

Why?

Keeper   All I wanted was good black coffee and a croissant.

H.D.   Why?

Domesticated Woman   To break my heart.

Keeper   Choice does not come into this equation as Einstein said in 1937.

H.D.   Was my father a good man, Mother?

Keeper   I have never been partial to reassembling the pieces of a vase after it has been broken. The truth is in the fragments. (*To* **Mourner**.) And then you arrived wanting to put the fragments together and ruined my peace . . .

H.D.   Was he? Was he a good man?

Keeper   He was a hierarchial man. Vertical in body and vertical in mind.

Domesticated Woman   An intelligent soft-spoken man. It wasn't his fault the world is like it is. We live in barbaric times. You make everything so complicated.

Pause.

He had very smooth hands. Cool clean shirts.

H.D.   Are you my mother?

Domesticated Woman   No, darling. But I very much wanted to be.

H.D. (*to* **Keeper**)   Did you want to be?

Keeper   Oh I'm very very tired. (*She starts to sleep.*)

H.D. *runs to her fishing bucket and pours a bucketful of water and seaweed over* **Keeper**.

Keeper (*jolted awake*)   Your papa, H.D., was an
uncritical receiver of orders. He bred a master race of
blond brutes to serve the Fatherland. To do this he
needed bodies to experiment on. And he did. (*She
picks the seaweed from her clothes and face.*) He was a
geneticist. A clever man. He made paté out of duck
livers for breakfast.

H.D.   Was I grown in a teacup? Was I?

Keeper   His job was to fashion the human shape.
Build the human equivalent of Nuremberg stadium.
To plant embryos into the wombs of Aryan women and
make them grow into blocks of stone. She's right
(**Domesticated Woman**.) – your womb *is* your wealth.
I did not want to end up like your rabbit. Nor do
I want to end up with a bucket of seaweed over me
when I'm in pain.

H.D.   I don't know what's going on. I'm only three
inches big. Perhaps the cigars have stunted my growth.
Or was he a small man? (*To* **Keeper**.) Sorry. (**Keeper**
pushes her away.)

Domesticated Woman   He had broad shoulders and
came from a good family. Your father and I were in
love, darling.

Keeper   My family were abolished. I watched their
smoke rage from the chimneys. But we won't dwell on
ash. Your father helped me escape.

Domesticated Woman   Human nature is a terrible
thing.

Keeper   My breasts were firm. Charisma is a good
ointment to tuck into your brassiere when death fondles
your nipple. I had an elegant tongue and elegant thighs
. . . and vasn't I lucky!

Domesticated Woman   I sympathise with everyone.

Keeper I made love with your father eight times.
I counted. You were not grown in a teacup.

H.D. Why didn't you abort me? Oh, I don't know
a fish from an egg!

Keeper I wanted you. I wanted you very badly.
I wanted a child and I wanted you.

H.D. Oh.

Keeper I wanted you when I smuggled you over
borders in a hatbox . . . I wanted you when the chief of
police stroked my cheek and offered me a visa . . .
I wanted you when I was hungry and cold . . . I wanted
you in railway stations . . . in interrogation rooms . . . in
strangers' beds . . . I wanted you in crowds . . . in
doorways . . . in cafés . . . I wanted you and have never
regretted you . . . my virgin daughter . . . ten fingers and
toes . . . skin clear as water . . . a perfect little girl . . .
born under a bridge.

Domesticated Woman Why do you have to ruin
everything?

H.D. Why did you hide me away?

Domesticated Woman You look just like him. She's
ashamed.

Keeper Your father was a very famous man. And he
confessed you. I did not want you to become a political
pet. For the media and biographer.

Domesticated Woman He must have suffered
terribly. He hung himself.

H.D. From an oak? Or a pine?

Domesticated Woman We were engaged to be
married. I still have the ring. (*Pause.*) Ruby.

H.D. (*sings*)
  And if that mocking bird don't sing
  Mama's going to buy you a ruby ring . . .

Pause.

Daddy. Speak to me. Fascist Daddy, gentle Daddy.
Handsome doctor Daddy. I want him to speak to me!

Mourner I never knew my father. I found something
in my pocket. Here. (*She gives it to* **H.D.**)

H.D. What is it?

Mourner A pea.

Domesticated Woman Darling, do you always carry
peas around with you? I'll give you a nice lipstick to
keep in your pocket instead.

Mourner The first experiment in genetics was done
on a pea.

H.D. I'm a pea. Nothing but a pea!

Keeper Let me make this clear to you, my daughter.
Your father never wore jackboots. Never hung up flags.
Never sang patriotic songs. The military mind has to be
formed. Your father was a scientist not a military man.
He had a melancholy nature.

H.D. ME! SPEAK TO ME!

Keeper I have seen progress cripple itself and have no
hope for your young bones.

H.D. ME!

Domesticated Woman We'll kill the Russians better
than they can kill us!

Keeper Oh, go and gargle Cola and then stuff your
pillow case with popcorn!

Domesticated Woman Did he love me?

H.D.   Did he love her?

Keeper   Perhaps he loved Willheim Schmidt best.
A chicken farmer and astrologer. Carried out mass
murders without flinching. Yes, he loved Willheim best.
Rubbed his shoulders after a hard day's massacre. Ran
him a bath.

Domesticated Woman   Your father sent me flowers
every day.

Keeper   Enough for all the graves in Europe.

Domesticated Woman   To think of all the years
I thought about him. Dreamt about him. Imagined my
husband was him.

Keeper   He told me you made a mouth-watering
apple strudel.

Domesticated Woman (*tears*)   I've been burgled!

H.D.   Have I read about my white-coated Daddy?
Have I come across him in books?

Keeper   He wrote nothing down. He gave oral reports
to his colleagues. Words make pictures. Jawbones. Eye
sockets. Ovaries. But he did leave something. He left me
money and he left you the criminal calendar of Europe.

H.D.   I'm off, Mama. (*Lights a cigar.*) I don't want your
money and I don't want his calendar.

Keeper   I take it with lemon today.

Mourner   I should probably go home too.

Keeper   Who's going to wind the clock?

H.D.   My silver-haired mother.

Keeper   Are these tears? Or pearls? Or is this
a Jacobean tragedy? The stage is littered with corpses.

(*Pause.*) My hair will knot. Become quite unmanageable.

H.D. (*leaving*) Don't forget to water the cabbages.

H.D. *kisses her mother. Gives her cigar to* **Mourner** *who takes a puff and then coughs violently. She is studying a bone she has found. Gives it to* **Keeper**.

Keeper Ah. Poor Fritz. He was a goot dog.

H.D. *exits.* **Mourner** *follows her.*

Scene Four

Sound of **Mourner** *sobbing.*

H.D. *creeps across the stage and snips the second bud from* **Domesticated Woman**'s *plant.* **H.D.** *stands over* **Mourner**'s *bed, holding the bud.*

H.D. Why do you cry all the time?

Mourner I'm scared.

H.D. What are you scared of?

Mourner Don't know. The future. (*Sobs.*) I don't know how to ... to ... to make the things ... the things I want happen.

A helicopter flies noisily overhead.

H.D. I'm scared too. And I'm cold. I can't play the piano any more.

Mourner What are you scared of?

H.D. The past. It's getting in the way of things.

Pause.

And I'll miss my mother's horrible, sarcastic lips.

She exits holding the bud.

Scene Five

Domesticated Woman *walks to her plant. She screams.*

Domesticated Woman   My sons! Someone has snipped my sons!

H.D. *enters.*

H.D.   I nipped them in the bud.

Domesticated Woman   But I watered them every day!

H.D.   I left you the farmer. I like people who can make things grow.

Scene Six

Night.

Keeper *lights an opium pipe.* **Domesticated Woman** *sits painting her fingernails.*

Keeper (*holding up the pipe*)   A present from Madame Mao. I find it relieves stress when my ideological spine needs relaxing. When the footbinder came to break her toes – she threw herself in the river. I met her on a small wooden boat. The sun was blood red. (*She lights the pipe and puffs.*)

Domesticated Woman   I used to wear poppy-pink in those days.

Keeper   Ah poppies!

Domesticated Woman   With lipstick to match.

Keeper *hands the opium pipe to* **Domesticated Woman**.

Domesticated Woman   What do I do?

Keeper Breathe.

Domesticated Woman Breathe?

Keeper In and out?

Domesticated Woman *takes the pipe tentatively. Inhales.*
Coughs. Inhales again.

Domesticated Woman (*takes off her shoes*) My ankles
are swollen with water. Retained. The doctor has to give
me diuretics. My husband says he'll drain them when
the drought comes.

Keeper Is he a comedian?

Domesticated Woman No. He's a sadist.

They start laughing.

I wanted my sons to be ballet dancers. To move with
grace and beauty. They're built like tanks!

Keeper So's my daughter!

They both laugh even more.

Domesticated Woman Just before I left to come
here I went on a picnic with Sarah-Jo. I baked flapjacks
and she brought raspberry wine. We walked in the
woods . . . it was a very hot day . . . and as no one was
there . . . we took off all our clothes and jumped into
the stream.

Pause.

Keeper Vell?

Domesticated Woman I saw Sarah-Jo's body . . . it
was covered in bruises. I know her and Dan . . . (*Pause.*)
. . . you see she has a daughter . . . and I have noticed
that she also . . . when she wears sleeveless dresses . . .
the thing is *I like* Sarah-Jo . . . I don't like to think she

might be hurt ... (*Briskly.*) ... There now ... what
came over me? I have noticed that your house is full of
dust and you're putting on weight!

Keeper (*by her globe*)   If I could have shaped the world
rather than merely survived it ... I would have stressed
the need for human beings to show their care and
concern for each other freely. (*She spins the globe.*) There
I am. With dust in my belly button. And my daughter
making her way in the world without me.

Scene Seven

Day.

Mourner's *departure.*
Mourner *takes down her clothes and packs them in a box. She
switches on the tape recorder and listens to her recording as
she packs.*

Tape   Seventy million years ago, at the close of the
cretaceous, the earth was devastated. After its passing,
there was no large animal left in existence. The few
remaining birds, mammals, reptiles and land plants, saw
a drastic reduction in their numbers. They inherited an
earth that would have seemed empty ...

Keeper   I vant to go back to Vienna.

Tape   In the last few years of its dominion, the
dinosaur was subjected to unbearable pressure. That
much we know. (*Pause.*) That much I know. With their
hormonal systems hopelessly out of balance they left us
a clue to the agony they must have suffered. (*Pause.*) The
clue is in the eggs they left behind ... A symptom of
their stress, the eggs started to get thinner and thinner
... the embryo could not get enough calcium to build
up its skeleton. That much I know ... (*Pause.*) ... Those

that did go through the ordeal of being laid ... were born old ... appearing from the shells with faces and bodies wrinkled with age ... the fate of their offspring was sealed.

H.D.'s *voice comes on the tape.*

H.D.   I have left you a map. You will find it in the pocket of your white coat.

Mourner *goes to the white coat, feels in the pocket, takes out the map. She unfolds it and reads:*

H.D.   'If you want to find me you can. Where I am is very cold, harassed, uncertain, but never lonely. I will teach you to make a fire and walk long distances. H.D.'

Mourner *takes down the white coat and packs it. She switches off the tape. She makes her way over to* **Keeper** *carrying the box and her suitcase and hands the suitcase to* **Keeper**.

Keeper   *Moi?*

Mourner   You said you never had one.

Keeper   Ah. True. Thank you. You can see my hair has turned quite silver with gratitude.

Mourner (*to* **Domesticated Woman**)   I've got something for you too. (*She fumbles in her box. She hands a wrapped-up object to* **Domesticated Woman**.)

Domesticated Woman (*unwraps it*)   An egg?

Mourner   I've kept it warm. You must do the same.

Domesticated Woman   Is there something inside it?

Keeper   Is there intelligence inside it?

Mourner   You must keep it warm.

Domesticated Woman   Well. Thank you. (*She smiles. She wraps up the egg safely.*) I'll keep it secret. Perhaps next time I'll see some of your creatures in the museum.

Mourner *leaves.*

Domesticated Woman (*to* **Keeper**) What's going
to become of them both? Of us? What if they become
communists? (**Keeper** *starts to laugh.*) . . . Education is the
responsibility of the parent . . . we've both failed . . .
utterly . . . (*She sobs.*) . . . I'd love a quarter-pounder and
some French fries.

She sobs more. **Keeper** *laughs more.*

Why are you always so superior? Always making me feel
dumb? If I complained I'd have nowhere to live. I've
got no money of my own . . . I had to scrub floors to
pay my fare . . . my back still aches . . . (*She sobs.*)

Keeper I will rub it with eucalyptus and warm a brick
for your bed.

Domesticated Woman That would really be very
nice . . . and then I must pack . . . (*She sobs.*)

Keeper If blood appears when I prick my finger I'll
write you a letter.

Domesticated Woman Don't make me cry. There
would be no reason ever to stop . . . (*She stifles her sobs.*)
. . . I try not to cry in the daytime . . . it's vulgar . . .

Keeper My pillows are always damp.

Domesticated Woman My back aches so . . .

Keeper Eucalyptus!

Domesticated Woman *and* **Keeper** *stand up.* **Keeper**
is holding the hairbrush. She looks at **Domesticated**
Woman *and as* **Domesticated Woman** *looks back, hands
her the hairbrush.* **Domesticated Woman** *brushes her hair
gently, then leaves.*

Scene Eight

Night.

Keeper *onstage with lamps and globes lit.*
Domesticated Woman's *wig is on the head of the Madonna.*
Keeper *is covering the objects onstage with a white cloth as she speaks.*
Soft piano music.

Keeper   When I returned to Berlin in 19 . . . the cabarets were still playing . . . but the political jokes were veiled and whispered . . . theatres were still open . . . but they performed safe classics . . . concert halls had lost their best performers to television . . . books had been censored or destroyed . . . galleries were full of empty spaces where 'degenerate' art had been removed . . .

Pause.

So what's changed?
I'm glad I saw Paris before they built the skyscrapers.
I'm glad I saw Bologna before they turned the river into a gravel pit.

She puts a white cloth over the buddha.

I wish I'd been to India . . . and Africa . . .

She stops and looks over the white-covered objects.

All this white. Looks like leukaemia.

She goes and sits by the globe.

My advice to the young used to be . . . not to hurry.
Now I'm not so sure. (*Pause.*) . . . But then to express dissatisfaction with life at the age of one hundred and

ninety years old ... is a little ungracious ... don't you think?

Lights fade but the globe remains lit.

End.

Clam

Clam was first presented by Blood Group at the Oval House Theatre, London, on 25 April 1985, with the following cast:

Alice/Nadia Krupskaya/Patient   Miné Kaylan
Harry/Vladimir Lenin/Doctor   Andrzey
Borkowski

Director Anna Furse
Designers Deborah Levy and Anna Furse

Characters

A man and a woman play:
Harry and **Alice**
Vladimir Lenin and **Nadia Krupskaya**
Doctor and **Patient**

Set

Table
One large chair/one small chair
One large mug/one small mug
Fish tank

Scene One

*In which **Alice** and **Harry** discuss distance.*

Table.
*One large tin mug (**Harry**'s).*
*One small china cup and saucer (**Alice**'s).*
*One large chair (**Harry**'s).*
*One small chair (**Alice**'s).*
Teapot.
Large fish tank. Dominant.
Harry *wears a top hat with dollar label stuck on it, and white kid gloves.*
Alice *wears a scarlet puffed sleeved dress and black patent leather shoes.*
Harry *pours tea. First, a lot into the little china cup, and then a little into the big tin mug. He hands the cup and saucer to **Alice**.*

Alice   Thank you, Harry.

Harry   I wish it was a pleasure, Alice. (*Lifting the mug.*) My fingers. Prematurely arthritic. Sad.

Alice   Your fingers probed my heart ... quite carelessly ... in those days.

Harry   (*sipping tea*)   But it's all very calm now.

Alice   Yes.

Harry   The joints. I have to crack each knuckle when I wake up in the mornings. I feel ridiculous. (*He laughs.*)

Alice   Shame.

Harry   Oh, it's all right. Don't worry about me.

Alice   I don't.

Both sip tea.

Cold.

Harry   Lukewarm.

Alice   But a comforting ritual nevertheless.

Pause.

Harry   I suppose you'll want to know the time?

Alice   I try not to think about it.

Harry   It's very close indeed. (*He searches the table.*) Too close for comfort. I can taste it in my tea. (*He searches the teapot. He takes out a watch on a chain.*) Thought so. Two hands. That point to numbers. That measure out our day. I loved your hands.

Alice   I've still got them.

Harry   We forget . . . in the measuring out of moments . . . that there . . . there are . . .

Alice   Clues.

Harry   To explain distance.

They swap chairs.

A beginning and an end . . . measured out by these two hands . . . they could be East and West . . .

Alice   They could be me and you . . .

Harry   A beginning and an end that might not be . . .

Alice   Resolved.

Pause.

Would you like a clam with your tea?

Harry   It's just what I feel like right now.

Alice *walks to the fishtank. She puts her arm into the water, swishes around.* **Harry** *watches. He grimaces with every swish.* **Alice** *triumphantly pulls out a clam. Brief interlude of Schiller's*

'Ode to Joy', played very loud. She puts it on the small china plate and hands it to **Harry**.

Harry   Thank you, Alice.

Alice   I wish it was a pleasure, Harry.

Harry *cracks the clam.*

Harry   There's not even the desire to hurt one another.

Alice   No. (*The sound of the clam cracking.*) If I was far away from you, say we were separated by an ocean . . . any ocean . . . I would even write you letters.

Harry   And I would reply. And take great care how I replied.

Alice   I would look forward to that.

Harry   I know you would.

Alice   I might even think of you if I saw something in a shop I know you would like. Or send you a book. Or remember to tell you something someone had said to me. Or find some shoes . . . size nine . . . your size . . . and buy them for you . . . or a postcard with an image that would mean something to you . . . or look at a sculpture and imagine how you would see it . . .

Harry   And it would not cause either of us to feel pain.

Pause.

Alice   Harry?

Harry   Yes?

Alice   What would you do if something you really didn't want to see . . . flew two inches above your head?

Harry   Duck.

Scene Two

In which **Lenin** *and* **Nadia** *discuss lust.*

Fish tank. Two 'fish' swim sublimely. A duck quacks off.

Lenin   Nadia Krupskaya! Why do you keep your husband waiting like this?

Nadia (*off*)   I am plucking a duck, Vladimir.

Lenin (*pacing*)   A duck? My Nadia is plucking a duck ... and I am gathering my thoughts in order to address two thousand spirit-gutted comrades in five minutes ... a carefully drawn-up plan on how best reform can be achieved in the sixth wing of the ...

Nadia *enters wearing a tiara of feathers.*

Lenin (*staggers*)   You want to give me a revolutionary heart attack? My wife dressed like a bourgeois peacock ...

Nadia   A tiara made from *duck*, Vladimir.

Lenin   Strutting before my far-seeing and penetrating eyes like a tipsy czarina ... *Nadia*!

Nadia   Kiss me, Vladimir.

Lenin (*collecting himself*)   I will shake your hand in a friendly manner. And then you will remove your foolish finery and accompany your husband like an honest wife ... instead of a clucking foul who has lost all reason.

Nadia   Oh, *Vladimir*! That our hearts might be banners of *unreason* just once. For they are good hearts ... pumping victorious and glorious as our machines ... a little lustful oil ... Vladimir ...

Lenin *strides to the fish tank. He takes a mouthful of water. He gargles. Spits. The water turns red.*

Lenin   I wash your mouth out for you, Nadia. You

make a mockery of the struggle . . . of science . . . for
what is scientific is truth and can never be criticised . . .

Nadia   Let me *feel* science then, Vladimir . . . dab
science on my nipples, on my period pains, on my pulse
points . . . on the small of my back . . .

Pause.

Lenin   Nadia. You are not well. I feel compassion and
will be tender with you for one minute. (*He takes a watch
on a chain from his pocket, checks it, puts it back, walks to her.*)

Nadia   A little closer, Vladimir.

He embraces her stiffly.

Aaaaah. Vladimir . . . you have strong arms for a man
who works so much with his head . . . Vladimir . . . if
. . . if . . . just once we could maybe pack a picnic and
eat black bread in the pine forest . . . or sit on the
balcony drinking lemon tea . . . perhaps playing chess
. . . and although we were silent . . . it would be . . . you
might even cook me something . . . soup or a little salt
beef with horseradish . . . you might even lose yourself
a little . . . intoxicate your clear thinking with the Black
Sea smell of my hair . . .

Lenin (*pulls away from her*)   I prefer the honest smell of
dung . . . the gentle sigh of dialectic. You are in need of
re-education. I am looking at a sick woman.

Nadia   *Look* at me then.

He looks at her piercingly.

S W O O N!

Lenin   Swoon? You are asking a man who has rocked
the world with the most significant social change this
century has witnessed . . . to swoon?

Nadia   Yes.

Pause.

Swooooooon.

Pause.

S W O O O O O N!!!

Lenin (*takes out a red hanky, wipes his brow*)   I . . . I . . .
I . . .

He staggers.

Nadia   MORE! More swoon.

Lenin   I . . . I . . . I . . . (*Staggering more.*) What do you
want from me, Nadia?

Nadia   I want swoon.

Lenin (*staggers to the fish tank*)   What . . . what you
understand subjectively as swoon . . . does not matter . . .
What matters is the objective logic of class relations in
affairs of swoon . . .

Nadia *leaps towards him. She sticks his head under the water of
the fish tank. She holds him under.*

Nadia   Then I will have to find a young comrade to
explore this 'objective swoon' with . . . for short-lived
passion is more poetic and pure than the dry kisses of
doctrine . . . we will explore ideology between the legs
and in the armpit . . .

Lenin (*surfacing*)   Nadia? Why do you put goldfish in
the samovar?

Nadia   It was a wicked aberration of the imagination,
Vladimir.

Lenin   I frown like the furrows we plough in our
frozen fields, my wife. We are talking about revolution
not imagination.

Nadia   Imagination, Vladimir, like revolution, has a 't' in it.

Lenin   You are a sick woman. I look upon you as a doctor would his patient.

Scene Three

In which **Doctor** *and* **Patient** *explore nonsense.*

Patient *is horizontal.*

Patient   Doctor, I am a sick woman.

Doctor   You say you have pains in your stomach, Patient?

Patient   I need to be rehabilitated.

Doctor   Locate your symphony and begin.

Patient   Day by day my discerning senses are being numbed. I have come to the conclusion this is not a personal disability but an international conspiracy.

Doctor   (*quickly holds up four fingers*)   How many internationals am I holding up?

Patient   Your wife.

The lights dim. Spot on **Doctor**. *He addresses the audience.*

Doctor   Gentlemen, the case I have to place before you today is a curious one. Not only does the patient insist she is a woman, she insists she is a Russian woman. When she continued to insist I stuck a needle through her forehead. She seems genuinely distressed and is plainly a danger to herself, so I placed clamps on her wrists and negotiated short electric spasms through her skull by placing electric wires on her forehead. The patient does not seem to worry in the least about her surroundings.

Spot switches to **Patient**.

Patient   Dear Alice, he told me I was insane and
irrational. Then he stuck a needle through my forehead.
Then he put clamps on my wrists. Then he put electric
wires on my temple and burnt some of my hair. Love,
Nadia.

Patient *and* **Doctor** *resume treatment.*

Doctor   Do you have a particular association
with helicopters?

Patient   The army.

Doctor   Are you frightened of the army?

Patient   I'm frightened of you too.

Doctor *plucks a feather from her tiara. She winces.*

Patient   Do you think we were born cruel, Doctor?

Doctor   Yes.

They both cry loudly and inconsolably. They suddenly stop.

Do you think we were born kind, loving and full of
need, Patient?

Patient   Yes.

They both laugh loudly and hollowly.

Doctor   So tell me something I haven't heard before?

Scene Four

In which **Alice** *and* **Harry** *find clues.*

Darkness.
The sound of water splashing.
Alice *and* **Harry** *sit by the fish tank which is full of all kinds*
of objects: i.e., a brush, comb, shoes, a bible, an orange, cigarettes,

a necklace, the complete works of Shakespeare, a Union Jack,
sweets . . . etc.
They take it in turns to fish things out of the tank and name them.

Harry Oh, look! I've just found a dinosaur's knee cap!

Alice And I've found a dinosaur's elbow!

Harry Is it a knuckle?

Alice No it's a gas chamber.

Harry Tell me a story, Alice.

Alice You're bound to tell me you've heard it
all before.

Harry Then I'll find it reassuring. Is this
an apartheid?

Alice No it's a fathom. Which reminds me. Last week
I went for a walk across twenty-five miles of a beach
forbidden to me . . .

Harry Think I've found an et cetera . . .

Alice No. That's a Cumbria. Or it could be
a clandestine.

Pause.

Do you know what I found there, Harry?

Harry Mohammedanism?

Alice Extinct creatures. Scattered across the rocks and
shingle . . . creatures that would never geographically
survive there . . . I found things under shrubs . . . that
should never have been there . . .

Harry Pearls?

Alice A tapir . . . a bit like a lizard . . . all the way
from Venezuela . . . perhaps Ecuador or Columbia . . .
its mouth open and under its tongue little bits of

decaying fruit and shoots from trees . . . as if it had
predicted its own extinction . . . a *yak* . . . Harry, I found
a dead yak . . . all the way from the tundra . . . lying on
its back by a bush . . . further on . . . nearer the rock
pools I found a rhino . . . its head was severed from its
body . . . the horn removed . . . piles of excrement
scattered across the reeds . . . I kept walking . . . must
have done about eight miles by now . . . saw something
peeping out of the sand . . . an eye . . . the pupil was
white so I knew whatever it was was blind . . . I dug
with my hands . . . the sand soft as butter . . . an *antelope*,
Harry . . . beautiful black patches on its forehead . . . it
had been shot there too . . . the bullet still lodged in the
flesh and bone . . .

Harry   Is this an idiosyncracy?

Alice   Looks like a broody. (*Pause.*) The sea was very
calm that day . . . grey-green . . . I stood close to the
shore enjoying the air and wind . . . bent down to pick
up a stone . . . saw the last of the creatures . . . there by
my feet . . . I remember reading about it . . . oh years
before I met you . . . a *tuatara* . . . like a small dragon
with tiny strings on its chest . . . known as the sting
carrier . . . and by it . . . a whole clutter of unhatched
eggs . . . some buried in the mud . . . covered with salt
crystals . . . they just lay there . . . so hopeful . . . paper-
thin shells . . . I put my hand to my head and found
some of my hair was falling out . . . and I began to
wonder, Harry, whether I was becoming extinct . . . put
my hands down my pants . . . discovered blood on my
fingers . . . just a little . . . nothing to worry about.

Harry   I'd like to make a sculpture of you, Alice.

Alice   I vomited into the sea . . . quite suddenly . . .
and I had this *vision*, Harry . . . watching the patterns
my vomit made with the waves . . . The whole of
Eastern Europe . . . much of it extinct . . . came in with

the tide ... Poland ... Latvia ... Lithuania ...
Hungary ... Czechoslovakia ... dropped on our
poisoned shores ... and thousands of people ran out to
look ... children with buckets and spades ... adults in
sun hats ... teenagers with radios hugged to their ears
... shopkeepers ... ice-cream sellers ... all stood in
silence just looking ... for a long time ... until some
began to touch ... turned Romania on its side and
began to feel it ... a little boy pissed on the Ukraine
... a woman in a bikini put Poland on her belly ...
placed her lover's hand there too ... an old man buried
his head in Lithuania and wept ... And then I saw
further out ... just a speck on the sea, *India* ...
stranded ... babies with khol-blacked eyes gashed
themselves on the rocks ... a yoghurt-maker's ladle
bobbed up and down ... lilies ... cucumber ... fennel
... aniseed ... churned with the waves ...

Harry   I've just found another rabbit hole.

Alice   And I another laxative.

Harry   Is it evangelical?

Alice   Nor is it a lake.

Pause.

Kiss me, Harry.

Pause.

Harry   You see, Alice, if you walked twenty-five miles
along a radioactive beach, it would not be a good idea
to kiss you.

Very loud and brief rendering of 'Ode to Joy'.

Scene Five

*In which **Doctor** and **Patient** discuss 'The Enemy'.*

Doctor *is eating a carrot fished up from the tank in the previous scene.*

Patient   It's not a very good idea to eat that carrot.

Doctor   Oh?

He continues to eat with more relish.

Why's that?

Patient   It was washed up on the shores of a radioactive beach.

Doctor   I see.

Patient   It might send you a bit funny.

Doctor   Really?

A pause as he chews and thinks.

The diagnosis? I think you are severely disillusioned. Bitter. Twisted. Titter. Bwisted. Twitter. Blistered. Bwittered. Twitterered.

This can go on for some time as he goes 'funny'.

The prescription? Years of imprisonment. Phone tapping. Mounted police. Electric shocks. I suppose you want to know the time? Teatime. (*He picks objects up from the floor.*) So who cares about the cholesterol? Will you partake in a *petit bourgeois*? Do you hate me, Patient?

Scene Six

In which **Alice** *and* **Harry** *discuss aesthetics.*

Harry *in a big chair.*
Alice *in a little chair.*

Alice   Are you still fond of me, Harry?

Harry   If I was to involve myself in relation to an object, let's say a sculptural involvement as I am a

sculptor ... and was asked to choreograph myself into
one of my exhibitions ... I could do a number of
things. I could stand in relation to shape, weight,
texture, height, scale, colour. I would have to decide
whether I wanted to make my body shape similar to the
object ... or contrast myself with it. Feeling and
psychology would not come into the equation. Unless
I was interested in descriptive gesture. But then I'm not
interested in being profound or polemic or a catalyst for
social change. Merely presenting a sequence of
abstracted movement.

They swap chairs.

Alice   If you were talking to me about love I would
listen to you and while you were talking I would see
that you were observing the angle of my hand in
relation to the window frame, or the poised fingers of
a woman smoking a cigarette in relation to the blue
curtains, or the plastic milk carton in relation to the
porcelain jar from Britanny containing mead which
being very sweet you might contrast with three withered
lemons juxtaposed by chance at an interesting angle in
relation to an old woman with withered breasts whose
ankles might be interesting in relation to the four legs
of the green straw chair ... not forgetting the window
frame in relation to the whole composition.

The swap chairs.

Would you like a clam without your tea, Harry?

Harry   Thank you, Alice. That's just what I feel like
right now.

Scene Seven

In which **Doctor** *and* **Patient** *discuss love.*

Doctor (*plucking feathers*)   She loves me, she loves me not, she loves me she loves me she loves me not she loves me . . .

Patient   I would like to love you.

Doctor   I would like you to love me.

Patient   I would like you to love me.

Doctor   I would like to think you could love me and I could love you.

Patient   I would like that.

Doctor   What would it take?

Patient   Could you take this bullet out of my chest?

Scene Eight

In which **Harry** *gives an interview.*

Harry *sits alone. Teaset laid out for one. He wears hat and gloves as in Scene One. He looks straight out.*

Harry   I'm sorry Alice got shot. (*He pours tea.*) But I'm glad an American soldier shot her and not a Brit. No, I don't think she had a death wish. In fact she was pregnant. Yes, she was a close friend of mine and I'll miss her. I am at the moment exhibiting my most recent sculptures and have called the composition 'Women at War'. It explores this whole question of civil disobedience. Since the tragic incident I have been commissioned to write a short essay on the subject for an eminent publishing house.

Pause.

It feels strange drinking tea alone.

He sips tea.

She would have made a very good mother. Poor Alice and her unhatched egg.

Scene Nine

In which **Nadia Krupskaya** *and* **Vladimir Lenin** *discuss what is to be done.*
Lenin *paces the floor. He is irate.*

Lenin   NADIA KRUPSKAYA!

Pause.

NADIA!

Nadia (*off*)   I am plucking a poet, Vladimir.

Lenin   A poet? HA! I suppose he tells you the sky is yellow and the grass pink ... whispers sweet pumpkin cake verse in your ear ... HA! If he opened his mouth ... what would come out ... a sugar lump? A little philosophy ... something he picked up on a tram? Borscht without Beetroot. Nadia! Come to your husband!

Nadia   C.O.M.I.N.G.

Lenin *takes out a watch on a chain. He paces.*

Lenin   Why does my heart beat like this? Very fast. All week I have felt ... tearful ... my dreams are unspeakable ... one gets the feeling ... there is so little time ... time for what, I ask? My shoes pinch ... twice I have loosened my collar, my lip twitches ... hands shake ... It is not good for the morale of my people to show fear ... weakness ... and then I think ... to acknowledge the fear ... maybe ... to voice the

unspeakable . . . might be a good thing . . . to have
achieved so much . . . so huge a task . . . so many
sacrifices . . . Our people . . . opened their hearts to
change . . . and it happened . . . we built ourselves
a future . . . out of nothing . . . problems . . . many
problems . . . we said we could not achieve everything at
once . . . we made mistakes . . . and the West laughed at
us . . . relished our every stumble . . . trod on our young
bones . . . but against all the odds . . . considerable odds
. . . we grew . . . put our faith and blood in what was
right . . . I had vision and they came with me . . . they
had muscle and they used it . . . and now to think . . .
our great bear . . . once half starved, limping, chained
. . . now with a good coat of fur, bright eyes, Russian
eyes . . . might not . . . bear cubs . . . or will give birth
to mutant beasts with three heads . . . is this a tear,
Vladimir? . . . am I weeping like a child? . . . to think
we conquered feudalism . . . slavery . . . for this . . .

Nadia *enters in bra and pants.*

Lenin Nadia . . .

Nadia Yes, Vladimir?

Lenin Nadia . . . I need . . . I need to empty
my bladder.

Nadia Vladimir, would you like a clam with your tea
or are you trying to tell me something?

Brief burst of 'Ode to Joy'.

End.

1990s, Identity: Post-Modern Knots

The B File

Introduction

The B File was created in response to a workshop I was asked to write and direct for the Magdalena Project in Cardiff (October 1991).

The theme of my choice was to find a theatrical version/translation of some of the ideas I was exploring in my fiction *Swallowing Geography*. I used fragments of this text as ideas to depart from and framed the workshop with three questions:

1. B is feeling homesick in her own home. Where does she want to be?
2. B is missing someone she's never met. Who is this person?
3. B wants to be someone else. Who does she want to be?

'She is the wanderer, bum, émigré, refugee, deportee, strolling player. Sometimes she would like to be a settler, but curiosity, grief and disaffection forbid the unpacking of her bags.

B is searching for home.

She smokes a cigarette bought at a small kiosk while changing trains at the last border she crossed. A border is an undefined margin between two things; sanity and insanity, for example. It is an edge. To be marginal is to be not fully defined. This thought excites her.

"Who are you?" X asks, watching her put heavy gold hoops into her ears. "I am a country disguised and made up, offering itself to tourists." ' (*Swallowing Geography*)

I was interested in the yearning for a place and a person never met. An imagined place or half-imagined person. The familiar feeling of knowing you want things to be different (less bleak, less reduced, less lonely), having a fragmented picture in the mind of what that might be, an atmosphere or a·moment, but not knowing how to meet it. Not knowing how to make the things you want happen.

The melancholy and the solace of daydreams.

The B File, an erotic interrogation, premiered at Chapter
Arts, Cardiff in November 1992.

Characters

Beatrice One
Beatrice Two
Beatrice Three
Beatrice Four
Beatrice Five
(written as **B1, B2, B3, B4, B5**)

Props

Two microphones and five suitcases.

Note

Three of the performers in the version of *The B File*
speak Welsh, Italian and Greek. This, of course, can
change in subsequent performances according to the
languages performers speak – with the proviso that 'The
Interpreter' always translates. The physical/
choreographic possibilities of five bodies on stage are
obvious to performers and director. I have not noted in
detail what I chose to do in this version of *The B File*
except to say that there were very formal ensemble
choreographic sequences, sometimes a duet and, at
times, one Beatrice mirrored the gesture of another.

The five **Beatrices**, *suitcases in their hands, lean or sit on the sides of the stage. They sip cans of Pepsi, eat a sandwich, consider the audience coming in, take out tissues to wipe hands, etc.*

The stage fills with blue light.

They assemble on stage and sing in harmony the words:

All   God is dead.

Exit with suitcases to the sides of the stage except for **B1**. **B5** *walks to the microphone and becomes the* **Interpreter**.

Spotlight on **B1**.

Interpreter   She says look at me.

B1 *points to her tongue, her finger, the back of her knee.*

Interpreter   She says look.

B1   My name is B.

Interpreter   She says her name is Beatrice. Beatrice knows three sentences in Welsh.

B1   Rwyn dy garu di canad.

Interpreter   She says, I love you, darling.

B1   Elsian mynd ir qwelly dy ti.

Interpreter   She says, I want to go to bed with you.

B1   Cia'r drivs.

Interpreter   She says, shut the door.
Is Beatrice a character?
If she is a Welsh character, is she dressed for the part?
Is Beatrice a persona?
If she is a Welsh persona, what are her voices?

B2 *walks to the microphone and gives it to* **B1**.

B1   What do you do to make people love you?

B2 *whispers something in her ear.*

B1 (*surprised*)   Oh.

B2 *exits to side of stage.*

B1 (*into microphone to audience*)   I do cheap things to make people like me. I make them feel more important than they are and flatter them, and when someone makes me a great cocktail I take a sip and shout . . .

B2 (*interrupts*)   Dragonflies!

B1 (*smiles*)   Dragonflies. What's your name, my sweet? Is it Jonny or Sam or Brett or Julie or Mandy or Linda? I'd like to go down on you and for you to talk to me about football and religion and hamburgers and what it feels like to come. Do you feel safe? Or do you feel alone and scared? When you feel fear does it have detail or is it just a force? Baby, do you sometimes feel glum? Baby, take care of yourself. Oh baby, I'd like to stroke you and whisper things to you and make you not feel fear.

(*To* **Beatrices**.) Are you happy with your life, my sweet? Is home a good place? Or just somewhere to return to? Are you pleased to open your eyes in the morning? What do you see?

(*To audience*.) Oh my love, let me call you that – my love – let us imagine what that means . . . you and I lip-locked some place in the American South. You and I in a motor on the highway making plans for the future. The radio is on and we hear the Soviet Union has come apart . . . just come apart. People wake up and don't know what country they're in. Children make new cities from snow . . . name them . . . and un-name them and . . . then there are some ads for Pepsi and bagel chips, and back to a war in Yugoslavia. And all the time we are hot for each other. Through all this world news we just want to be in each other's pants. And we pull in for gas and I'm saying – no, baby, don't light a cigarette

right now, wait till we pull out and anyhow we'll check
into a motel soon – hey, darling, I'm imagining
America! It's all from magazines and movies, I'm hot for
you and I've found America! We're stuffing fries and
ketchup into each other's mouths and, baby, you're so
hard . . .

Pause.

Honey . . . I'm thinking of all the people I've jilted
meanly. And all the people who've dumped me – my
pockets are full of old bills and tickets . . . and my heart
is busting with love.

Interpreter   Who are you?

B1   My name is Beatrice. I am wearing a black dress,
black shoes, red lipstick and my hair up. I live with my
husband X and I have a cat.

Interpreter   Do you love X?

B1   Yes.

Interpreter   Does X love you?

B1   Yes.

Interpreter   What words do you say to X when you
make love?

B1   Honey, sweetheart, baby, darling.

Interpreter   What kind of effect do you want your
words to have?

Pause.

What kind of effect do you want your words to have?

B1   My husband and I have a secret. If we look at
each other, we'll die.

Interpreter   After you have made love, who goes to
sleep first?

B1   He does.

Interpreter   What do you think about while he sleeps?

B1   Fuck off.

Pause.

Interpreter   Tell me about your day.

B1   Today we got a postcard from Beatrice. A picture of desert sand and white thorns. All day I have been imagining the desert. And when I did my shopping I imagined Beatrice there.

Interpreter   But you are Beatrice.

B1   I know.

Pause.

Interpreter   She says she is feeling homesick in her own home.

Music.

All the **Beatrices** *look out in various states of restlessness.*

Music stops.

B4   Beatrice.

B1   Yes?

B4   Come here.

Pause.

B4   Why do you hate me?

B1   I don't.

B4   You do.

B1   I want you to be someone else.

Interpreter   Who is this person?

B1 *walks off calling for her cat.*

The stage fills with blue light.

All the **Beatrices** *assemble in a line*
In unison they open their suitcases.
We hear the birdsong of paradise.

B1 (*sings*)
  How can I work like other women do?
  How can I work when the sky's so blue?

All exit to the sides of the stage.

B2 *stands in spotlight. She is heavily pregnant.*
Dark glasses. Raunchy. Silent.

Interpreter   She says look at me.

Pause.

She says look.

Pause.

She says look.

Pause.

She says her name is Beatrice.
Is Beatrice a character?
If she is a pregnant character, is she dressed for the
part?
Is Beatrice a persona?
If she is a pregnant persona, what are her voices?

One of the **Beatrices** *gives her the microphone.*

B2 (*sings. Belts out*)
  Do-re-eeeen
  Don't make me wait until tomorrow
  No-oo No-oo
  Please let me love you tonite
  And it will be al-rite

You can't make me say I don't want you
No-o No-o
My heart is burning with love
And I want you tonite

Interpreter   Who are you?

B2   My name is Beatrice. I am wearing a black dress, black shoes, black tattooOOO, crystal necklace, my hair UP and red lipstick.

Interpreter   Do you love the father of your child?

B2   No.

Interpreter   Does the father of your child love you?

B2   No.

Interpreter   What words do you say to the father of your child when you make love?

B2   We don't make love.

Interpreter   What words do you say to the father of your child when you fuck?

B2   I don't say words.

Interpreter   After you fuck who goes to sleep first?

B2   He does.

Interpreter   What do you think about while he sleeps?

B2 *walks off.*
Stops.
Sings almost like the Koran.

B2 (*sings*)
    Take me h-i-g-h-e-r.

Blackout.

All the **Beatrices** *line up with suitcases.*

They hold them up so that the following slides can be projected on to them.

1. *A wall with the words 'Nothing Is Happening' written across it.*
2. *A white vest.*
3. *A map.*
4. *A stamped addressed airmail envelope.*
5. *Ships in a harbour.*

Lights.

B3 *stands in spotlight.*

B3   Guarda mi.

Interpreter   She says, look at me.

B3 (*points to her hands, her back, her feet*)   Guarda. Guarda. Guarda.

Interpreter   She says, look. Look. Look.
Beatrice knows three sentences in Italian.

B3   Uno.

Interpreter   One.

B3   Che cosafainella vita?

Interpreter   What do you do in life?

B3   Due.

Interpreter   Two.

B3   Sei sposato?

Interpreter   Are you married?

B3   Tre.

Interpreter   Three.

B3   Mio padre fa del vino bellissimo.

Interpreter   She says, my father makes beautiful wine.

Is Beatrice a character?
If she is a character, is she dressed for the part?
Is Beatrice a persona?
If she is a persona, what are her voices?

One of the **Beatrices** *gives her a microphone.*

B3   Gracias.

B4   My pleasure. (*Exits to the side.*)

B3   Mi manca la persona che non homai incontracto.

Interpreter   She says she is missing someone she has
never met. Who is this person?

B3 (*into microphone*)   This person is Beatrice.
Beatrice is wearing sandal shoes.
Beatrice is Spanish and . . .

Interpreter   But you are Italian.

B3   I know.

Music.

Music stops.

B3   Beatrice wears Yves St Laurent here. (*Points
to wrists.*)

Interpreter   What kind of effect do you want Yves St
Laurent to have?

B3   I want Yves St Laurent to give me a persona.
Beatrice is looking out of the window. She smokes
a cigarette. F-O-R-T-U-N-A. Someone stands behind
her. His name is Z. His hair is wet and he loves
Beatrice.
As she does him.
When she turns rund she knows he'll be there.
Her sandals are creaking.
Beatrice and Z are looking at ships in the harbour.

Music.

Music stops.

B3 Beatrice would like to stay for a while in the
same place.
Beatrice has a lot of regard for everybody.
But especially Z.
(*Soft.*) As he does her.
Beatrice would like to unpack her suitcase.

Music.

All the **Beatrices** *take one object out of their suitcases and
place it in the space. For example, a microwave; a picture of the
Pope/Ayatolloh; a compact disc player; a small computer; a
takeaway pizza box.*

B2's *object is a baby girl's dress.*

Music stops.

Interpreter Who are you?

B3 My name is B. I am wearing a blue dress, brown
shoes, red lipstick and my hair up.

Interpreter Do you love Z?

B3 Yes I do.

Interpreter Does Z love you?

B3 I hope.

Interpreter What words do you say to Z when you
make love?

B3 Tesoro.

Interpreter She says, my treasure.
What kind of effect do you want your words to have?

B3 Passione.

Interpreter She says, passion.

After you have made love who goes to sleep first?

B3 I do.

Interpreter What does Z think about while
you sleep?

B3 He takes a book and reads a map of the city.

Interpreter Beatrice is dreaming the city.

The stage fills with blue light.

B3 (*sings lament for the city*)
Pepsi Cola Smirnoff Tampax Esso Marmite Mitsubishi
Martini L'Oreal Holstein Persil Perrier Camel Lights

All (*sing*)
Pepsi Cola Smirnoff Tampax Esso Marmite Mitsubishi
Martini L'Oreal Holstein Persil Perrier Camel Lights.

All the **Beatrices** *assemble in a diagonal line, the heels of their
right shoes pointed out.*

B2 *eats a hamburger. She opens her suitcase. Inside it is a model
of a poor city park. A broken swing with a small child on it. She
pushes the swing.*

All the **Beatrices**' *fingers move, as if thinking through a
problem.*
Exit to the sides of the stage.

B4 *in spotlight.*
She touches her throat.

Interpreter She says, look at me.

B4 *touches her breast.*

Interpreter She says, look.

B4 My name is B.

Interpreter She says her name is Beatrice.
Beatrice knows three sentences in American.

B4   One.

Interpreter   One.

B4   Hey, man. Give me some skin.

Interpreter   She says, how do you do?

B4   Two.

Interpreter   Two.

B4   Oh, come on, babe.

Interpreter   She says, oh, come on, baby.

B4   Three.

Interpreter   Three

B4   It's time for the feet to hit the street.

Interpreter   She says, it's time to go.
Is Beatrice a character?
If she is an American character, is she dressed for
the part?
Is Beatrice a persona?
If she is an American persona, what are her voices?

One of the **Beatrices** *gives her a microphone.*

B4   (*into microphone*)   Yesterday I lost my spectacles so
today . . . although I can see big things . . . (*Turns to* **B3**.)
. . . I can see you, Beatrice . . . but I have to make up
detail. I can see you wearing a blue dress, yes I can see
that now you have your hand on your belly, on the
back of your neck, in your mouth, above your shoulder
. . . but Beatrice, I am having to make you up . . .
because at the moment you are just form . . . a female
shape in a blue dress and I think Beatrice that I will
keep you that way. I will keep you that way so I don't
have to meet you. Now you have turned to the side.
Are you inviting me to meet you? Or are you avoiding
me? This is a science, do you agree, Beatrice?

I can see your form in profile. I can see your neck. You wear your hair up and I am tempted to fill you in. I am tempted to colour you. You are saying ... the whole world loves fried food. Is this just a light-hearted observation, Beatrice? Are you making conversation? Or are you asking me to read between the lines? Are you asking me to consider not what you say, but how you say it?

Music.

Music stops.

You are saying ... today I bought a newspaper and it seemed to describe a world that doesn't fit me. Now you are embarrassed. You talk about a film you've seen instead. But I am not embarrassed. I ask you to continue. You are saying, when I unpack my suitcase it is to give myself narrative and biography. You are saying – today I will pack up the narrative and rearrange it somewhere else. In another capital city. In a small provincial town. In a lover's bedroom. (*Shouts.*) Why haven't you got a home, Beatrice?

Pause.

You are saying always cross the road like you got nine lives. But you haven't. You haven't. Are you a little suicidal? Or is it just bravado?

Music.

B4 *takes out a cigarette.*

B3 *walks over and lights it for her.*
They share it.

B4   I have put words into your mouth, Beatrice. Do my words fit you? If you are a persona I have revealed too much. If you are a character I have revealed too little. I have given you two possible moods. You are no longer just form. And I am curious. Perhaps I should

give you a physical action? You have a suitcase in your
hand. You are standing by a window. What are you
looking at? I can't see a harbour with ships in it. You
are looking at graffiti on a tower block. It says 'Nothing
Is Happening'.

You turn round. And there's nobody there.

B3   Z is there.

B4   No he isn't.

B3   I know.

Music.

Music stops.

B4   (*to* **B3**)   Who are you?

Pause.

Interpreter   Who are you?

B4   (*breaks open a lager*)   My name is Beatrice. I am
wearing a red dress, black patent shoes, red lipstick and
my hair up. (*Points to lager.*) Holstein.

Interpreter   Do you love your lovers?

B4   Sometimes.

Interpreter   Do your lovers love you?

B4   No.

Interpreter   What words do you say to your lovers
when you make love?

B4   Judith, Tess, Beatrice, Anna.

Interpreter   What effect do you want your words
to have?

B4   Operatic.

Interpreter   She says the effect she wants her words

to have is ideological. After you have made love who
goes to sleep first?

B4   She does.

Interpreter   What do you think about while
Judith sleeps?

B4   Tess.

Interpreter   What do you think about while
Tess sleeps?

B4   How to say goodbye.

Lights dim.

A slide of stones is projected on to the pregnant belly of **B2**.
One of the **Beatrices** *hands her the microphone.*
During the following dialogue we see **B2** *with a belly full of
stones. They travel up her body towards her heart.*

Interpreter   I've called to say goodbye.

B2   Goodbye.

Interpreter   Don't go without saying goodbye
properly.

B2   What does saying goodbye properly mean?

Pause.

Interpreter   Look I have to go. Can I call you later?

B2   I won't be here.

Interpreter   Where will you be?

Pause.

Give me a telephone number.

B2   Why haven't you asked me that before?

Interpreter   I have to go.

B2   Bye then.

Pause.

You forgot to ask a question. Is my unborn child
a persona?

She exits to side of stage.

Spotlight.

The **Interpreter** *picks up her large suitcase and walks into the*
spotlight. She is now **B5**. **B1** *also walks into the spotlight. They*
shake hands.

B5   How do you do?

B1   I have a little eczema on my wrists. (*Points.*) There.

B1 *picks up the large suitcase and walks to the microphone. She*
is now the **Interpreter**.

B5   Kitaxe me.

Interpreter   She says, look at me.

B5   Kita.

Touches her belly.

Kita.

Touches her arse.

Interpreter   She says, look.

B5   My name is Beatrice.

Interpreter   She says her name is Beatrice.
Beatrice knows three sentences in Greek.

B5   Ena.

Interpreter   One.

B5   Ma ti les tora?

Interpreter   She says, what are you talking about?

B5   Mas ta'pam kialz.

Interpreter   She says her fax number is 020 7477 6939.

B5   No. I said I've heard that story before.
Na parta.

Interpreter   She says, drop dead.
Is Beatrice a character?
If she is a Greek character, is she dressed for the part?
Is Beatrice a persona?
If she is a Greek persona, what are her voices?

B5   (*lifts arms above her head*)   Who am I now?

B5 *takes out a little green tissue.*
Dances a Greek dance.
Stops.

B5   Beatrice cleans offices at night with women in saris under orange strobe. She is eating dahl and chapatis in a room full of small rugs from Calcutta. She is playing the pinball machines with pimps and roughboys in arcades. Beatrice jangles her bracelets at borders. She flirts with blond boys in uniform and they give her a visa. Visas are her tattoos. She gathers plants and lists their medicinal properties using Latin names. Beatrice wants a garden. But she hasn't got one. Beatrice wants and wants. How is she going to make the things she wants happen?

Music.

All *the* **Beatrices** *shuffle, lean, stretch, blow their noses, cough, etc.*

Music stops.

B5   Beatrice is making international calls to her sister who is getting ready to go to Mass. She listens to her sister and she says, I carry a God-shaped suitcase around with me – that is the baggage you have given me. I am carrying the corpse of your superstition into the new century. And while she listens to her sister's reply, she mixes Martini with vodka bought at airports.

Looks at the objects on the floor.

B5   This is a shabby paradise. Beatrice is shooting up smack. Beatrice is storming heaven.

Music.

All the **Beatrices** *move their hands in fake Balinese soporific dance.*

Music stops.
Dancing stops.

B5   No. Beatrice is not shooting up smack. She is frying fish in Bologna. She takes out very clean white linen, unfolds it and sets the table for five . . .

B2 (*hands on her belly*)   Six.

B5   And she says to Beatrice 6, I cannot imagine a garden for you, my sweet. You will play in small city parks. You will cut your feet on glass and fall on dog shit. You will look at small deer through barbed wire and you will suck ice lollies in shopping malls.

The stage fills with blue light.

All the **Beatrices** *assemble with suitcases.*
They sing in harmony:

All   God is dead.

Interpreter   Who are you?

One of the **Beatrices** *hands her a microphone.*

B5   All right?

B3   I cut my finger . . . see?

B5   Oooh.

Interpreter   Who are you?

B3 *exits to side of stage.*

B5   My name is Beatrice. I am wearing a black dress, red shoes, red lipstick, gel to make my hair shine and I am growing a poppy in my window box.

Interpreter   Do you love your lovers?

B5   Georges?

Interpreter   She says, George.

B5   Ke ne ke ochi.

Interpreter   She says, yes and no.
Do your lovers love you?

B5   Ke ne ke ochi.

Interpreter   She says, yes and no.
What words do you say to your lovers when you make love?

B5   Matja mu.

Interpreter   She says, you are my eyes.
What kind of effect do you want your words to have?

B5 *makes a gesture.*

Interpreter   She says, drop dead.
After you have made love who goes to sleep first?

B5   Georges.

Interpreter   She says, George does. What do you think about while George sleeps?

Pause.

What do you think about while George sleeps?

B5   I think Beatrice is just an actress playing out what has been staged for her.

Music.

All the **Beatrices** *lift up their arms and click their fingers.*

Freeze.

B1 *walks downstage and unzips her dress.*
She stands naked with her back to the audience.

Blackout.

A slide of a very red poppy is projected on to her back.
Its green stem runs down her spine. She walks upstage and the
petals of the poppy spread across her shoulders and neck.

B1 (*sings. Very soft*)
   Take me hi-gher.

B2 (*sings. Very soft*)
   Take me hi-gh-er.

End.

Pushing the Prince into Denmark

Pushing the Prince into Denmark was originally written for Katherine Stark and Hilary Tones as a platform performance for the Royal Shakespeare Company, Stratford, in 1991.

Characters

Ophelia
Gertrude

Set

Two microphones, into which Gertrude and Ophelia speak.

A film is projected on to the stage. It is an image of a vast winter sky and snow falling. It plays throughout.

Ophelia wears woollen gloves on her hands.

Note

It seems to me that both Hamlet and Ophelia are constantly being told by the older folk to take their snot and tears elsewhere in Shakespeare's play. It is with this in mind that I make Gertrude insistently avoid Ophelia's attempt to articulate her unhappiness. Thus, in the repeated sequence when Gertrude says 'Stop it' to Ophelia, she means 'stop being sad'. Ophelia can only reply 'How?'

You will see that in this sequence there are directions for a tape of the Cocteau Twins to be played. The twins are two female singers who produce very gentle ambient music.

Fade in tape of the Cocteau Twins.
Fade in film of snow and sky.
Gertrude and **Ophelia** *take their positions by the microphones.*

Gertrude Stop it.

Ophelia How?

Gertrude Let it go.

Ophelia Where?

Gertrude Find other thoughts.

Ophelia How?

Gertrude Find them.

Ophelia Gone.

Gertrude Bring them back.

Ophelia Lost.

Gertrude Stop it.

Ophelia Can't.

Gertrude Find how.

Ophelia Tell me?

Pause.

Well then. Well then, I ask thee.

Tape fades.

Gertrude Everywhere is snow.
The trees are heavy with it. The sky is heavy with it.
It is the winter of discontent.
Today I wear velvet.
Today I feel beautiful.
Today I ate partridge for lunch.
Sweet Ophelia! The wind has gentled.

Ophelia (*whispers*)   You're a cunt, Gertrude.
Today we are at war.
Today I am hideous.
Every night I hear the ice crack.
Every night I fall asleep holding hot drinks to my chest.
I wake up wet because the drink has fallen from my
hand.
Even scalded I sleep.

Gertrude   If I sleep well and you are visited by
demons in your sleep, there is some melancholy in your
nature that needs demons.

Ophelia (*flat*)   There is some melancholy in your
nature that needs demons.

Gertrude (*hiccups*)   Partridge.
Undercooked.
My stomach hurts.
BUT THAT IS A PRIVATE MATTER!
I am looking out of the window and I can see that snow
is falling.

Ophelia   There are people sleeping out in the snow.
They are drunk and they are mad and they have run
away from their families.

Tape of the Cocteau Twins.

Gertrude   Stop it.

Ophelia   How?

Gertrude   Let it go.

Ophelia   Where?

Gertrude   Away.

Ophelia   Can't.

Gertrude   Away.

Ophelia   Can't.

Gertrude   Find how.

Ophelia   Tell me?

Pause.

Well then. Well then, I ask thee.

Tape fades.

Gertrude   Winter and war are harsh companions.
Today the wind turned over two ships. Men died. I did
not see this. It was reported to me. Tonight I will drink
wine with my husband. We will sit beside a fire of
burning pine and share the small incidents of the day.
We have bought property in Norway.

Ophelia (*flat*)   We have bought property in Norway.

Gertrude   Sweet Ophelia. The lake which has been
frozen for so long is now full of birds.

Ophelia (*whispers*)   Nine dead birds on the lake, you
halfwit.

Gertrude   Youth and beauty. Good reasons to wake
light-hearted.

Ophelia (*flat*)   To wake light-hearted.

Gertrude   Find other thoughts.

Ophelia   Where?

Gertrude   Find them.

Ophelia   Gone.

Gertrude   Bring them back.

Ophelia   Lost.

Gertrude   Here. My ring.
A gift. Take it.

Pause.

Take it.

Ophelia *crosses the stage to take it.*

Gertrude   No. Smile first.

Pause.

Smile. And then you can have it.

Fade in tape of the Cocteau Twins.
Lights fade on **Gertrude**. *Spot on* **Ophelia**.
Ophelia *opens her mouth.*
Slowly widens her lips.
Bares her teeth. Freezes.
Fade out tape. Fade out spot.

Gertrude   Take it.

Ophelia (*flat*)   Take it.

Gertrude   It is yours.

Ophelia   Smile first.

Pause.

Smile and then I will take it.

Fade in tape of the Cocteau Twins.
Lights fade on **Ophelia**. *Spot on* **Gertrude**.
Gertrude *opens her mouth.*
Slowly widens her lips
Bares her teeth. Freezes.
Fade out tape. Fade out spot.

Ophelia *walks back to her microphone without the ring.*

Ophelia   Is it true that we love? And then we do not
love? That we present affection and take it away again?

Gertrude   It is true that some love and others feel the
absence of love.

Ophelia   And others feel the absence of love.

Pause.

And is it true that if you are happy and someone else is not and you look out of the window at the same thing, you will see something quite different?

Gertrude   It is true that if I laugh and others weep, it is not I who took away their happiness.

Ophelia (*flat*)   It is not I who took away their happiness.

Gertrude   Stop it.

Ophelia   Stop it.

Gertrude   Let it go.

Ophelia   Where shall I go?

Gertrude   Away!

Ophelia   Away!
Where?
(*Points.*) This way? Or that way?

Tape of the Cocteau Twins.

Ophelia   There are daughters sleeping out in the snow. Their bodies have been forced to do things they do not want to do and they are sleeping in the snow.

Tape fades.

Gertrude   The days get dark early here. My ornamental pond has iced. The soldiers complain their blankets are too thin. All the servants have got a skin disease. I've given orders for them to wear long sleeves. I can feel the itch creep into my cheeks already. And mine is a face kissed by kings.

Ophelia (*flat*)   And mine is a face kissed by kings. Today I collected flowers on a walk.

Gertrude   Sweet Ophelia. A good reason to wake light-hearted.

Ophelia Something else happened on my walk. There was a little girl and she had gloves on her fingers. She was shutting a door. I turned round to call for her, and as I turned, she disappeared. She was there and then she was not there. She has gone missing. What place has she put herself in? I really must take care of myself. It is possible, Gertrude, that you and I get up now and look for her. We could look for her in the grass where the snow is thawing. We could want to find her, and the wanting will be a magnet to pull her to us. We could get up now and look for her, find the place she has put herself in, for it is not a comfortable place. And be with her.

Gertrude Be with her? Where is she?

Ophelia Lost. She is lost.

Gertrude If a small child gets lost, it is not I who gave her wrong directions.

Ophelia (*flat*) It is not I who gave her wrong directions.

Pause.

Something else happened.

Pause.

I turned round to call for her, and as I turned, she jumped. She lifted up her arms and jumped.

Sharp intake of breath.

Like that.

Tape of the Cocteau Twins.

Gertrude Stop it.

Ophelia How?

Gertrude   Let it go.

Ophelia   Where?

Gertrude   Away.

Ophelia   Can't.

Gertrude   Away.

Ophelia   Can't.

Gertrude   Find how.

Ophelia   Tell me.

Pause.

Well then. Well then, I ask thee.

Gertrude   Horses fall wounded on the ice. I did not
see this, it was reported to me. Every day a birth,
a wedding, something to make me smile. A pompous
courtier, my foolish puppy. Tonight I will take off my
velvet dress and lie naked with my king. Lip to lip we
will make heat to crack the frozen fiords. When I
pushed the prince into Denmark he screamed. And as
he screamed men were slaughtered. I have often wanted
to murder my son. To stop his breath as he lay in his
crib. To fill his screaming mouth with snow.

Pause.

Grief has no age.
Every day I made small fists with my hands.
But that is a private matter.

Ophelia (*flat*)   Much loved Gertrude.
Much kissed Gertrude.
Well fed Gertrude.
Well fucked Gertrude.

Gertrude   Youth and beauty and all she does is tear
at her pimples. Not a fit sight for the back of coins.

Ophelia (*flat*)   Not a fit sight for the back of coins.

Tape of the Cocteau Twins.

Gertrude   Stop it.

Ophelia   How?

Gertrude   Let it go.

Ophelia   Where?

Gertrude   Away.

Ophelia   Can't.

Gertrude   Away.

Ophelia (*points*)   This way? Or that way?

*Fade lights on **Ophelia** and **Gertrude**.*
We just see the film of the sky and snow falling.

End.

Honey, Baby

14 STUDIES IN EXILE

an investigation into the mix-up of five citizens in the contemporary world

Honey, Baby was first produced at LaMama Theatre, Melbourne, Australia, with the following cast:

Ella	Susannah Gregan
Pavel	Grant Moulday
Mary James	Victoria Eagger
Ernest James	Carlos Sanchez
Customs Official	Ian Scott

Directed by Suzanne Chaundry
Sound design by Roderick Poole
Video footage by Tomek Koman

Characters

The Lovers:
Ella
Pavel
They are dressed in fashionable, cosmopolitan gear. Clothes for fighting and flirting in.
Husband and Wife:
Mary James
Ernest James
They wear the uniform of rural Middle England. Mary James has her skirt caught in her knickers for most of the show — as if she forgot to hitch it down after the toilet. Her husband, being something of a sadist, has not pointed this out to her.
Customs Official
Written as **C.O.** *He wears appropriate uniform.*

Production Notes

The more culturally diverse the casting is, the better.

The music should be something contemporary with hybrid cultural references: Talvin Singh's 'Sounds From The Asian Underground' or his CD *OK* would be perfect.

Given that the play is structured around '14 STUDIES IN EXILE', the cast take it upon themselves to hold up cards (1–14) as appropriate. I have specified two places where the cards are held up by Mary James, the rest are up for grabs.

Note

Honey, Baby is an ensemble piece about cultural identity in contemporary Britain. I have attempted to bust open the word 'exile' and suggest that it is not just the experience of 'refugees' and 'asylum seekers' from elsewhere, but instead is most of our experience in the modern world.

Study in Exile No. 1

Ensemble enter.
C.O. *trickles some mustard on to a hot dog and eats.*
Lovers prepare their microphones.
Mary James *carries a placard. It says: 'Self-Raising Flour. Urgent.'*
Ernest James *carries a placard. It says: 'Donor'.*

Ernest I've got something on my mind. Something in the middle of my mind because I come from Middle England. I come from the middle and I need to say what's on my mind.

Mary Wait, Ernest. Wait your turn. The show has just began and it's not your turn.

Ernest My mind is full, Mary. It is full of things I need to say. I want to change the order. I want a new order. An order that starts with me standing in the centre of the stage.

Mary Yes. That was number one.

Ernest Was it? Good. I want to be number two as well.

Mary I want to be Marilyn Monroe.
You know, take lots of sleeping pills and die.

Music.

Study in Exile No. 2

The lovers talk into two microphones.

Pavel Call me baby.

Ella Baby.

Pause.

Call me honey.

Pavel　Honey.

Ella　Baby.

Pavel　Honey.

Ella　Baby.

Pavel　Honey, I want you to be someone else.

Ella　Who do you want me to be?

Pavel　Yes. That was number two.

Ella　Number two what?

Pavel　Study in exile number two.

Music.

Study in Exile No. 3

C.O. *places his hands on* **Ella**'s *head.*
Blue light.

C.O.　So. What have we here? Gotta lot of the
twentieth lurkin an a bit of the twenty-first. Nice to meet
you in the new century, babee! You got communist hair!
You full of red berries, girlie. You is Putin's daughter
cock-eyed on vodka. But you is from New Cross, how
come you got Russia lurking? Your daddy a commie?
Hey! You got Liz Taylor in here singing sleep songs
from the Betty Ford, sleeeeeep tight! Snot and tears in
here – man, there's segregation in here – black on this
bus white on that bus – yous Mr X's sister and you got
a dream . . . what happened to your dream, girl? All
muddled up in here. Your daddy leavin the house an he
don't come back to tell your mammy why. Him making
'nother home an more kiddies an now he's leaving that
home as well. Your daddy got many homes but no

home. He is not wise. Hey, you is a cybergirlie all
silicone and Silk Cut! You on the Internet you got
computer red-eye – whass happened to your spine, man,
you're talking dirty your name is Cindy you're doing a
calendar you love the Pope you're high on crack. No.
Uh uh. You aint Slavic. Mexican, maybe? Latino. Your
mammy Mexican? Love enchiladas myself, so's the wife.
Got a mammy?

Pause.

Where's my mammy?

Video:
Close-up of boiled egg being tapped by spoon.
Sound of a baby gurgling.
We see a mother and her baby son.
Mother slices top off egg.
Close-up of baby's mouth opening wide for spoon.

C.O. *lifts up* **Ella**'s *dress. We see her knickers.*

C.O.   I'm a lookin for someone who hurt me.

Ella   I am not her.

C.O.   You is.

Ella   I'm not.

C.O.   You are.

Ella   I'm not.

C.O.   You'll do. Wontcha mom?

Pause.

Call me baby.

Ella   Baby.

We hear the amplified sound of the boiled egg being tapped in the
film.
Ensemble stand in a number of restless and uncomfortable
positions:

Mary *writes 'Sultanas' on her placard.*
Ernest *rocks on his heels.*
Pavel *takes a blast from his asthma inhaler.*

C.O.   You let my daddy hit me and you never said a word.

Music.

Ella *walks back to microphones.*

Study in Exile No. 4

Ella   I've lost my front-door keys.

Pavel   Everything has a place. That's what you've got to remember. Then you won't lose things.

Ella   You're so different from me.

Pavel   Yes. That was number four.

Music.

Study in Exile No. 5

*In which **Mary** reveals it is possible to be homesick in her own home.*

Video:
Close-up of a suburban carpet. A dog being thrown biscuits. It catches them in its mouth. Sound of crunching as we see its molars.

Mary   A cold day but nice. This is a house. A lovely house. Birds sing. Oh how the birds sing! Starlings. Tits. Sparrows! How the English birds sing in my lovely garden so very green on account of the rain, the gentle but persistent rain that falls every day and makes indoors seem so inviting despite the twitch to stoop and dig my lovely garden whilst humming in English if you know what I mean (*whispers*) there's nothing wrong with my mind something is upsetting me deep down. (*Shouts at her husband.*) You trod on my crocuses!

Ernest Stand up straight when you speak in public. You're not sitting on the toilet.

Mary My husband thinks he's a chicken. I say, Ernest, even chickens have to wait their turn.

Ernest I do not think I'm a chicken. My wife is mad and has no problem displaying her condition to the nation.

Mary The doctor said have him committed. But I need the feathers! I need the feathers for our duvet because Ernest doesn't like continental feathers. He says they're dishonest and a bit slitty. 'Take my feathers and stuff the quilt,' he says, and that's what I do but when he eats prawns his feathers turn pink and I can't persuade him to eat pies which make a purple feather, yes a more lustrous feather so much easier on the eye when the quilt splits open and feathers fly.

Ernest Sing our song, Mary.

Mary (*sings*)
  What is life to me without thee?
  What is left if thou art dead?
  What is life without thee?
  What is life without my love?

Pause.

Ernest. I am so very homesick. I want to go home.

Ernest But you are in your home, Mary. I am your husband. Here is your sofa. There is your carpet. This is your shelving unit. Look out of the window. This is your view. This is your house.

This information makes **Mary** *weep into a tissue.*

Mary (*sobbing*) But it is not my home.

Ernest I'm waiting my turn, Mary, so don't take so long with your bit. I am your husband. Your life companion. And this *is* your home.

Mary (*whispers*) Call me Honey.

Ernest I can't.

Mary You have to. It's written in the play.

Ernest It's not English.

Mary Ernest, I'm going to make something up and while I do so you get yourself ready to say HONEY!

Smiles at audience.

The plumber once said, Look, Mary, look! Look how the sun makes your blue eyes shine! I said, I can't look, silly! How can I look at my own eyes?

Ernest (*pokes his throat*) It won't come through.

Chokes.

It won't come. Can't say it.

Mary *doesn't stop weeping until way into the next scene.*

The lovers.
They speak into microphones.

Pavel Honey.

Ella Baby.

Pavel Honey.

Ella Baby.

Pavel Honey, did you find your keys?

Ella (*whispers*) No.

Pavel (*whispers*)   Honey?

Ella   Yes?

Pavel   I want you to be someone else.

Ella   Who do you want me to be?

Pavel   I want you to be blonde. I want you to have blue eyes and American teeth.

Pause.

You wear a necklace made from turquoise glass and show me photos of yourself laughing in swimming pools. When I kiss you I can taste your perfume on my tongue. Dioressence. You have a small bruise on your upper arm, a bruise that is turning yellow. We are walking arm in arm across the boulevards of Western Europe, dizzy from too much coffee. You are wearing grey suede shoes and a watch, a watch that isn't fastened properly on your wrist. You are probably going to lose it. I like it that you don't care and time doesn't matter and that your wrists are small. We go to see a film. In the dark I circle your wrists with my fingers. Afterwards we eat seafood and whisper things of no consequence.

Ella (*whispers*)   But I'm not blonde.

Pavel   I know.

Ella   What are my words?

Pavel   I don't think you have words.

Pause.

You are just presence.

Pause.

You are sex.

Ella   What are my sex words?

Pavel   No words. It's in your body. Your body is all atmosphere. You never look me in the eye. If you do, your eyes move away, sleepy, somewhere else.

Ella   Do we fuck?

Pavel   Oh yes.

Pause.

Ella   What happens after?

Pavel   It's morning. We get dressed.

Ella   What happens between sex and morning?

Pavel   You say: when I was a little girl I was so light I could stand on my father's hand and he would lift me up to the ceiling.

Ella   Do you like that?

Pavel   Yes.

Ella   When I was a little girl I was so light I could stand on my father's hand and he would lift me up to the ceiling.

Pavel   Hmm. We pretend to sleep.

Ella   Where are we?

Pavel   A hotel. There's a Coke machine outside our door. We pretend to sleep while we listen to cans tumbling down the machine. People drink Coke and Fanta all night long.

Ella   It's morning.

Pavel   I kiss your bruise. I like it that you are perfect and that you are bruised.

Ella (*whispers*)   Baby, do you ever ask me why I am bruised?

Pavel   No. We get dressed and go.

Ella   Where do we go?

Pavel   I go to the airport. You go to the railway station.

Pause.

We exchange telephone numbers.

Ella   02 435 9976.

Pavel   0010 34 77 180.

Ella   Do we see each other again?

Ernest (*shouts*)   Who fucking cares? It's my turn! It's my bloody turn. Shut the fuck up and listen to me, Ernest James, bred in the middle with developed opinions and an endowment policy that has gone horribly wrong it's my turn to say what's on my mind.

Mary   It is actually. It really is his turn.

She holds up a card with 'No. 6' on it.
C.O., **Mary**, **Pavel**, **Ella** *gather round.*

Study in Exile No. 6

Ernest   It's in the middle of my mind because I live in Middle England and it's very very nice here in the middle but there are thoughts in the middle of my mind that I need to say to citizens who don't live in the middle but who might want to move here – it won't take long but it must be said remember you need my vote I have a firm and steady hand when inscribing my cross on a ballot. I carry a donor card but don't want my liver, kidneys, lungs or heart going to the gold-toothed over-educated sun-dried masala cunts and barely pale with oozing eyes and flaking feet, rancid hair oil and murderous children. I don't like their chest hair either. I regret to say I will not donate my organs to them. I invite my wife Mary James to support my opinions.

Ella *passes microphone to* **Pavel** *who passes it to* **C.O.** *who passes it to* **Mary**.

Mary   It is my husband's support in the face of so many odds that has steadied my nerves. I have a sense of belonging and being valued.

Music.

Study in Exile No. 7

C.O. *places his hands on* **Pavel**'s *head. Blue light.*

C.O.   Says here you're a male.

Pavel   Yes.

C.O.   Sure you're not Cuban? Gotta dick?

Pavel   Yes.

C.O.   So have a lotta Cubans. You think us actors are stoopid? But I can do a lot of voices, can't I? What have we got here? Yep. Calcutta! Yous got oxen bones poking through. How come, boy? Says here you waz born in Birmingham. You got some weird ceremony in this head. Yous got bent prophets in here! Wass happenin? Yous eating finger-lickin in Bollywood yous pumping iron in Archway – uh-oh you snorting snow with Suzie . . . Kuwait? What you doin in Kuwait? You spraying a limo . . . Seat belts on folk! You a lonely-heart box number yous at the football yous dancing with auntie – hey yous got new e-mail! Collect your electronic correspondence, sir! Yous walking down the boulevards of Barcelona with a girl she's lost her watch you kissing her wrist you drinking Fanta, man, you're putting on a condom yous eating noodles in heaven, boy! My! All jumbled up in here. Where does you come from, sad boy? A bit from here a bit from there. Your sister speak Urdu your brother speak French you shave with razors made in China – why (*Whispers.*) a razor is an implement – a torture gadget. Hey, you got sheep dung in here! Somethin from the Black Sea somethin lurking. You an Arab? Your grandma an Arab? Eh? Got a daddy?

Are you my daddy?

Pavel   No.

Video:
A father looks down at his small – five-year-old – son. Father scratches his ear, as if thinking about something. Son looks away. Father reveals that he is holding a strap in his hand. The child knows he is going to be beaten.

C.O.   I'm a lookin for someone to punish. Someone who hurt me.

Pavel   I am not him.

C.O.   You are.

Pavel   I'm not.

We hear the amplified sound of the boiled egg being tapped as in the film before. Ensemble of cast in various positions of silent and tense disquiet.

C.O.   Call me baby.

Pavel   Baby.

C.O.   You're giving me the evil eye, daddy-o.

Music.

Pavel *walks over to his microphone while taking a blast from his asthma inhaler.*

Study in Exile No. 8

Ella   Baby.

Pavel   Honey.

Pause.

Have you lost anything else?

Ella   Yes.

Pause.

I can't find my credit cards.

Pavel   At least you know what you've lost.

Pause.

I've lost something. But I don't know what it is.

Ella   That was number eight.

Music.

Study in Exile No. 9

Mary *holds a birthday cake with candles in one hand and a knife in the other.* **Ernest** *stands next to her wearing a paper party hat in the shape of an SM hood.*

Mary (*whispers, horrified*)   The cake! Candied peel! (*Ominous.*) Sultanas! Happy birthday, Ernest! You were born. Yes, Ernest, you were once born! You hatched in Hampshire.

Ernest   Surrey.

Mary   Don't apologise, Ernest. There's nothing wrong with Hampshire.

Ernest   My wife needs to see a discreet doctor but the

locum is an Indian who moved to the middle despite our agricultural community giving him the finger whilst feeding cows to cows believing as we do in same to same as you would to me and I to you.

Mary   Happy birthday, Ernest! First you blow out the candles. Don't singe your giblets I need them for the gravy.

Ernest *blows out candles.*

Mary   Well done! Now you cut the cake.

Holds the knife out to him.

Go on. Take it!

Ernest   Really? Are you sure?

Mary   You take the knife and cut the cake.

Ernest   I don't know about this.

Mary (*shouts*)   Cut the cake.

Ernest *takes the knife. Cuts the cake.*

Mary   Good! And now you make a wish. Shut your eyes.

Ernest *shuts his eyes still holding the knife.*

Mary   Both eyes, Ernest. That's right.

Ernest   I can't find a wish.

Mary   Go deeper, Ernest. There must be a wish in there.

Ernest   I'm going deeper, Mary.

Mary   Keep breathing, Ernest.

Ernest   I'm very deep now.

Mary   Tread the deep with your legs, Ernest. As if you're riding a bicycle.

Ernest (*panics*)   I don't like it in here, Mary . . . I want to come up.

Mary   Have you found a wish yet?

Ernest   I'm in too deep, Mary! Help me!

Screams in terror.

There's mud in my nostrils!

Mary   Sing our song, Ernest.

Ernest (*eyes shut tight while holding the knife*)
What is life to me without thee?
What is left if thou art dead?
What is life without thee?
What is life without my love?

Mary   I felt your wish.

Angry.

I felt it.

Ernest   I didn't mean to, Mary.

Takes off his paper hood and cries into it.

Mary   Your wish went right through my ribs.

Grabs the knife from him.

Music.

The lovers.
They speak into microphones.

Ella   Baby.

Pavel   Honey.

Ella   Baby.

Pavel   Honey.

Ella   I want you to be someone else.

Pavel   Who do you want me to be?

Ella   I want you to be wise.

Pavel   But I'm not wise.

Ella   I want you to be a father who loves his children. I want you to be faithful to me and always fancy me and respect and admire me.

Pavel   Where do we live?

Ella   The metropolis is cruel and speedy. But it is also safe. If we cheat on each other we can disappear with our broken hearts into the crowd.

Pavel   What are my words?

Ella   You say things like, 'Why do people always say "I love you" in a sad voice?'

Pavel   (*whispers*)   Honey, I don't want children.

Ella   I know.

Pause.

Pavel   Why do people always say I love you in a sad voice?

Ella   I'm very fond of you too.

Pavel   What colour are my eyes?

Ella   Green.

Pavel   My eyes are brown.

Ella   I know.

Pavel   And then what happens?

Ella   Your green eyes take me in. You mull things over in a wise manner.

Pavel   Why is your arm bruised? Why do you lose things all the time?

Ella   And your green eyes take me in. And you understand everything. Without me explaining.

Pavel   Where are we?

Ella   Number ten. By the way, I've lost my driving licence.

Ernest (*interrupts. Goes berserk*)   Do we care? No we do not! It's my turn anyway. You're absent-minded and we are supposed to find this interesting? We do not. It's a personal flaw, like a wart.

Mary   It is his turn actually.

She holds up card with 'No. 10' on it.

Is there a doctor in the house? I've been stabbed in the ribs by my husband.

Music.

Study in Exile No. 10

C.O. *places his hands on* **Ernest**'s *head.*
Blue light.

C.O.   Wass this? You got low-flying planes on the runway here – planes crashing all over the place you got suicide techniques in here! You holding teddy in the dorm – hey you got stuff on yer underpants. Missing yer mammy course you are yous only six you got cold baths and conkers in here gotta little doggie jus here frontal lobe zone, white hound, pink eyes winkin at ya – now don't get hysterical, my, yous bent as fuck yous biting your fingernails yous hunting deer you got a nightmare on the left zone yous caught on barbed wire World War

One – or is that your pappy? – gotta clot in ya belly is
that colon cancer or is it kedgeree? Hey, just here, you
got three prostitutes in here, luvlies all of em they sayin
something – hi my name is Vivian take your time I'm
wet moist available take your time.

Video:
A bedroom. Door closes. Father leaves the room, strap in his hand.
Small son sobs into pillow.

C.O.   I am looking for someone to torture.

Ernest   I am Ernest James. From the middle. I live in
the middle of England.

C.O.   You'll do.

Ernest   Thank you.

Ernest *kisses* **C.O.** *full on the mouth.*

C.O.   Take your time.

More kissing.

Call me baby.

Ernest   Baby.

C.O.   Honey.

Ernest   Baby.

Pause.

May I ask you why you speak in those voices?

C.O.   I got em from cartoon network. Lost my voice
see. I'm an Essex boy but damned if I know howz to
speak Essex. Hollered when my pappy whacked me. Bin
Bugs Buggy ever since.

Takes a hot dog out of his pocket.

Honey. Do you want to share my hot dog?

Music.

Study in Exile No. 11

The lovers.
They speak into microphones.

Pavel   Honey.

Ella   Baby.

Pavel   Did you find your driving licence?

Ella   Someone else found it. And gave it back to me.

Pavel   Who?

Ella   A stranger.

Pavel   A man?

Ella   Yes.

Pavel   How did you say goodbye?

Ella   We discovered we were wearing the same shoes.

Pavel   But he's a man.

Ella   I wear men's shoes.

Pavel   Do you?

Ella   Yes.

Pavel   I'm jealous.

Ella   Why?

Pavel   Because he shares something with you that I don't.

Ella   Yes, that was number eleven.

Music.

Study in Exile No. 12

C.O. *puts his hand on* **Mary**'*s head.*
Blue light.

C.O.   Name? Place of birth? Father's place of birth?
Mother's place of birth?

Pause.

The loss of memory. Blankness. No recollection. Lapse.
Disremembered. On the tip of your tongue. (*Shakes his
fingers.*) Hey! I feel kinda dizzy! Think you might have
some minerals in your head and they kinda charged my
hand. Does the European community know about those
minerals? If you've crossed some zone I don't know
about I want to see your papers.

Pause.

English mustard, English beef, English beer, English
butter, English oblivion. OK something easy. Do you
have a daytime telephone number should I need to
contact you urgently?

Mary   072 662546.

CO   Where's that?

Mary *shakes her head.*

Ernest (*through a tannoy*)   Mary! We live in the middle
of England. This is your home. I am your husband.
Time to bath the dog and lick stamps.

Mary *shakes her head.*

Ernest   But, Mary, we're the same. We know who we
are. We know what we like and when to tap the
barometer!

Mary *shakes her head.*

Ernest   Mary. I've been meaning to tell you for some

time now ... um ... er ... well ... it's like this, Mary. (*Coughs.*) You've caught your skirt in your knickers.

Mary, *horrified, adjusts her skirt.*

Mary (*screams*) You hideous wet-lipped kike! You should have told me earlier.

Ernest (*screams*) I'm not a kike!

Mary You are!

Ernest I'm not!

Mary A hooked-nose sallow-skinned kike!

Ernest I'm pale. Barely yellow at all!

Mary You are!

Ernest I'm not!

Music.

Study in Exile No. 13

The lovers.
They speak into microphones.

Pavel We all live in the same world.

Ella We don't.

Pavel What then?

Pause.

Ella We're all the same underneath.

Pavel We're not.

Ella What then?

Pause.

I've lost you.

Pavel   Yes. That is number thirteen.

Ella   Baby.

Pavel   Honey.

Ella   Baby.

Music.

Study in Exile No. 14

Ernest   My mind is full, Mary. It is full of things I need to say.

Mary   Wait, Ernest. Wait your turn. The show is ending and it's not your turn.

Ernest   I want to change the order. An order that ends with me standing in the centre of the stage.

Mary   Yes. That was number fourteen.

Ernest   Standing in the middle here in Middle England waxing my chair whilst thinking of sodomy and damp leaves in the middle of England.

Video:
Close-up of a suburban carpet. A dog being thrown biscuits. It catches them in its mouth. Sound of crunching as we see its molars.

C.O.   *holds up a placard. It says: 'ERNIE – MEET ME AFTER THE SHOW.'*

Music.

End.

2000, The Loss of God and Politics

Macbeth – False Memories

Note

When I started writing *Macbeth – False Memories*, I realised that for those of us who are not Shakespeare scholars, the original play is like a memory we carry inside us, but we are not too sure of the details. Although I was not remotely interested in a contemporary adaptation of Shakespeare's play – a *Yo! Macbeth!* on roller skates – I wanted the characters in my play to carry some of the memories of the original, in the same way that we are all haunted by events from the past. There are three themes I have lifted from the original play. One, it is children who revenge their parents' murderers; two, a murdered man comes back as a ghost; three, although there is no Birnam Wood in my text – that is to say men pretending to be trees – I do explore the idea of camouflage. I have left out the theme of ambition. I think Bennet and his wife kill because they want to *feel* something – maybe they like to feel the intense terror of their victims. When I finished writing my *Macbeth*, I was left with a lingering feeling that Bennet and his wife resemble the son and daughter of Shakespeare's Macbeth and Lady Macbeth. It is as if they have inherited the nervous tics and twitches of their parents.

Macbeth – False Memories explores how a story told five hundred years ago travels into the concrete, pollution and speed of the twenty-first century.

Macbeth — False Memories was commissioned by the Actors Touring Company. It was first performed at the Waterman's Arts Centre, on 9 March 2000 prior to a national tour. The cast was as follows:

Bennet   Jonathan Lermit
Bennet's Wife   Tilly Edwards
Lavelli   Mario Vernazza
Lavelli's Daughter   Myriam Acharki
Tan/Michael   Khan Bonfils

Director, Nick Philippou
Assistant Director, Rebecca Manson Jones
Composer, Jeremy Peyton Jones
Designer and Lighting Designer, Zerlina Hughes
Costumes, Emma Davis
Stage Manager, Patricia Davenport

Characters

Bennet, *businessman, about forty.*
Bennet's Wife, *in her early twenties.*
Senor Lavelli, *an Italian businessman, about forty. He wears Armani or Versace, of course.*
Lavelli's Daughter, *in her early twenties. She is a stylish, high-maintenance Italian woman.*

Characters for the film

Bennet
Bennet's Wife
Senor Lavelli
Lavelli's Daughter
Waiter, *Asian. Early twenties. Beautiful.*
Three five-year-old **Girls**

Production note

Within the live theatre event is a film. This film carries most of the narrative. There are of course multiple opportunities for the film and the live theatre event to interact – in addition to the scenes written in the text.

Theatre Scene 1

Bennet's Wife *crosses the stage. She wears a white nightdress and carries a man's coat and shoes.* **Lavelli***'s ghost follows her.*

Blackout.

Fade in film:
Exterior. Woods.
Three five-year-old **Girls** *stare unblinkingly from the screen. They wear Elizabethan 'dressing-up-box' costumes and hairstyles. The three* **Girls** *open their mouths but no sound comes out. They are mouthing the word 'tomorrow'.*

Lavelli's Daughter (*voice-over*) I said I am so lonely it sometimes feels like I have come to the end of my life. I eat alone, drink alone, walk alone, sleep alone. Is it possible to feel alive if you have not been touched for two years?

Pause.

I'm becoming sad, disconnected from intimate pleasure . . . my father was the only person to see this, 'It's in your hands,' he said before he left Rome, 'your fingers are cold.' He said that in England people are kind and that all English gardens look like graveyards.

Pause.

I feel I'm getting closer to you, Mr Bennet.

The lights find **Bennet**. *He holds a mobile phone to his ear.* **Bennet** *wears a pinstriped suit. We see him in the shadows looking at the three* **Girls**.

Film Scene 1

Interior. Italian restaurant. UK.
The end of a large meal.
Close-up of **Lavelli**'s *teeth.*
Lavelli *smiling.*

Lavelli (*slowly, as if learning English*)   Today is Thurs-day. Tomorrow Fri-day.

Smiling **Waiter** *slams two espressos down.*

Lavelli (*speaks fast*)   When I was seventeen I took a pin and scratched my name into the skin of my arm. L-A-V-E-L-L-I. As if by writing my name in blood I would get to know myself better. Still I do not know who the real Lavelli is! And neither does my daughter. She likes to think I am nicer than I am.

Bennet *smiles weakly.*

Lavelli   She always says when are you coming to see me? And I say tomorrow! *Domani*! She has made of her father a forgery – a man who is more like the father she wants than the real thing. I'm a fake!

Lavelli *knocks back his espresso in one.*
Bennet *sips slowly.*

Lavelli   So. I have built a business around my fatal flaw. Show me a credit card and I will tell you in seconds if it is a forgery. The artist may correct his canvas fifty times, but the forger, if he is good, corrects his imitation only twice. He has to paint 'in the manner' of the original. And I have some respect for him. Those of us who cannot imitate, lack imagination. We cannot see outside our own manner . . . we are nasty little nationalists.

Waiter *stands behind* **Lavelli**. *Hands him the bill.* **Lavelli** *grabs* **Waiter**'s *hand and keeps hold of it while he speaks.*

Lavelli The foreigner, the stranger, he too must learn to make a forgery of himself. He must imitate the host culture. We are supposed to value originality, but the truth is we want to be like each other. We even want our differences to be the same differences. You still with me, Bennet?

Bennet Um. Yes.

Lavelli I need an investor who likes to get out of bed in the morning and who wants to make money. Money is a passion like collecting shoes. Money makes me squeeze my buttocks together with joy. For the last year my research staff have been using the design principle of butterfly wings to detect fraudulent goods.

Lavelli *flamboyantly gives credit card to* **Waiter**.

Bennet Why butterflies?

Lavelli Moths as well. Like certain butterflies, the moth is very good at camouflage. Butterflies are . . . uplifting. They raise the spirits.

Bennet (*flat*) Really.

Lavelli Yees!

Waiter *returns credit card to* **Lavelli**.

Waiter In Japan there are insects that look exactly like blossom.

Lavelli Yes! And somewhere there is an insect that looks exactly like Michael.

Bennet I will prepare some figures for our next meeting.

Waiter (*to* **Lavelli**) Do you want a taxi to your hotel?

Waiter *stands very close behind* **Lavelli**'*s chair*.

Lavelli Thank you, Tan!

Bennet   I thought his name was Michael?

Lavelli (*grinning*)   Are you Michael or are you Tan?

Waiter   In Canada I was Michael. Here I am
something else.

Lavelli   Yeees. (*To* **Bennet**.) Give my regards to your
beautiful young wife.

Theatre Scene 2

Lights find **Bennet**'s *young wife. She wears a white nightdress
and clutches a pillow.* **Lavelli**'s *ghost watches her. His Armani
suit is spattered with blood and he wipes his hands with a white
sheet. She screams. He imitates her scream.*

Lavelli   No. That is not absolutely right. A bad
forgery. I try again.

He screams.

Bellissima. (*Smiling.*) Dying is nothing. Anyone can
murder. The clever thing is to know how to make
people disappear.

*He throws the white sheet over her face so that with her white
dress she is completely camouflaged.*

Theatre Scene 3

The lights find **Bennet**. *A mobile hugged to his ear.*

Lavelli's Daughter (*voice-over*)   You say you have lost
all sensation in your fingertips?

Bennet   Yes.

Lavelli's Daughter   Can you feel anything?

Bennet   No. The right side of my face is numb.

Lavelli's Daughter Why is that, Bennet?

Bennet Where are you?

Lavelli's Daughter Rome.

Bennet I don't want you to call me again.

Lavelli's Daughter But you are talking to me on my father's telephone. Where is he, Bennet?

Bennet *examines his mobile.*

Theatre Scene 4

Bennet's Wife *takes the sheet off her face.*
She stares at **Lavelli**.

Lavelli I know you are not interested in camouflage or disguise. You want to be noticed. That is what you want more than anything else. But for someone who wants to be regarded you are strangely concealed. You are dim. You are not in the light. Your narcissism has made you fade. You have no presence. No charisma.

Surveys her.

You are blonde. I always say it is a crumbling man who likes blonde. He wants a child, a good girl who is chaste and fragile but who is also a lustful woman. Say after me, she must look like the fragrant flower . . .

Bennet's Wife She must look like the fragrant flower . . .

Lavelli But she must be the serpent underneath it.

Bennet's Wife But she must be the serpent underneath it.

Lavelli Yees. Not a bad forgery. I think I will be God. We will make you together. But what is it we are

making? What do you have a talent for? I think we are
making a murderess ... you have terror inside you ...
that is good ... you cannot murder without terror. I
give you a tip ... always drink a lot of water when you
bury the dead ... it will help you sweat. The actress
and the murderess have something in common. We
want to look at her, but more we want to look inside
her. Say after me, 'If you look at me you'll die.'

Bennet's Wife (*whispers*)   If you look at me you'll die.

Lavelli   I'm already dead. Your husband murdered me
because he wants to feel something.

Film Scene 2

Interior. Italian restaurant. UK.
Close-up of **Lavelli** *picking his teeth.*
He is reading **Bennet**'s *document which is open on the table.*
Bennet *walks towards him.*
Lavelli *kisses* **Bennet** *on both cheeks.*

Lavelli   Your wife is well?

Waiter *slams espresso and glass of water on table.*

Bennet   Yes, my wife is well.

Waiter *and* **Lavelli** *watch* **Bennet** *swallow his pills with*
water. Close-up of **Bennet**'s *face. He looks haunted.*

Lavelli (*smiling*)   But you are sick?

Bennet   The right side of my face is dead. (*Pinches his*
cheek.) Nothing. You've read my document?

Lavelli   It's a shame for you. Not to feel the lips of
your young wife ... just here.

Strokes **Bennet**'s *cheek. Scrutinises the business documents.*

Yes, of course I've read your document. I like your mathematics. Everything ends in three.

Laughs flirtatiously. **Bennet** *looks bemused.*

See. I have a little eczema here.

He parts hair. Points to forehead. There is nothing there. **Waiter** *watches.*

Bennet I can't see it.

Waiter When he is excited you can see it.

Lavelli And when I am anxious you can see it. I get the eczema my doctor says because I feel too much. This is a good business partnership then? You need to feel more. I need to feel less. So I am happy for you to take your five per cent. I will meet with my sponsors in Rome with this in mind.

Bennet It is always a pleasure to do business with you.

Grinning, **Lavelli** *stands up.* **Waiter** *helps him put on his expensive cashmere coat.* **Lavelli** *takes something out of his coat pocket. A small package wrapped in tissue paper. Hands it to* **Waiter**.

Lavelli A goodbye present.

He kisses **Waiter** *on mouth.*

(*To* **Bennet**) So. You'll drive me to the airport?

Theatre Scene 5

Bennet *hugs the mobile to ear. He sips a can of lager.*

Lavelli's Daughter (*voice-over*) You said you can't remember what you ever looked forward to or what is

precious to you. You said you don't know what you
believe in or why belief matters.

Pause.

Could you speak up please?

Bennet   I said I can't remember what I ever looked
forward to or what is precious to me. I don't know what
I am supposed to feel connected to. Nor do I want to
feel unconnected. I appreciate that I have to find my
own point to life and that there is not a higher being or
supernatural force that will give me a point . . .

Pause.

Lavelli's Daughter   You said you appreciate you
have to find your own point to life.

Bennet   I said I am having some difficulty finding the
point. I think I was once interested in politics . . . but I
can't remember what I valued above something else . . .
I cannot connect myself to it . . . it sounds far away . . .
round the block, your voice sounds nearer than that,
nearer than right and wrong and evil and good.

Lavelli's Daughter   You said you love your wife.

Bennet (*flat*)   Yes.

Lavelli's Daughter   But you said you have no
dreams?

Fade in film:
Interior. Woods.
Three five-year-old **Girls**. *They wear Elizabethan costumes and
hairstyles. They stare unblinkingly from the screen during his
speech.*

Girls (*sing*)   'Tomorrow! Tomorrow! Tomorrow!'

Bennet (*soft*)   I said I have no dreams.

Theatre Scene 6

Bennet's Wife. *She has changed a little under* **Lavelli***'s tutorship. Her lips are glossed red. Her hair resembles a 1930s Hollywood screen goddess.*

Bennet's Wife   A dream. My mother knocks on the door. She is dressed in a gold fake-fur lionskin. Her mouth is big. Gaping. She rolls on her back. Suddenly her big paws clasp me to her nylon fur breasts.

Lavelli*'s ghost listens, arms folded.*

Lavelli   Your dream is telling you that paradise is synthetic. The breast your mother pulls you to is made from nylon. Paradise is a forgery. Chin up. Good. Lengthen your limbs. Remember, I want to look at you, but more I want to look inside you. So the murderess must learn to make her eyes appear to be open when in truth she has shut the window and drawn the curtains. Don't forget to breathe.

Film Scene 3

Interior. Leather upholstered car.
Bennet *smokes a cigarette while he drives. He is incredibly nervous.*

Lavelli   Today is Satur-day. Tomorrow is Sunday.

Lavelli *is amused at the spectacle of himself pretending to learn English. Digs into his coat pocket. Unwraps a salami roll. Bites into it with gusto. He eats with his mouth open. Rolls the salami on his tongue. Spits out crumbs while he speaks.*

If your face is numb take a sauna. Heat is good for the stiff English spine.

The car comes to an abrupt stop.

Is there a problem?

Lavelli *wipes the crumbs off his face with a silk handkerchief exactly the same colour as his shirt.*

Theatre Scene 7

Lights find **Bennet***. A mobile hugged to his ear, he drinks a can of lager.*

Lavelli's Daughter (*voice-over*) How is it that I have ended up so very solo, Bennet? Am I more alone than anyone else or are they just better at concealing it? I have no lover, no garden, no child.

Bennet Why are you telling me this?

Lavelli's Daughter Because you want to know what is on Lavelli's daughter's mind. And what's on my mind, Bennet, are the facts of life. But I have to go now. Business. I am meeting with my father's researchers today. Did you know that the monarch butterfly has a magnetic substance in its body? In autumn, when it migrates from America to Mexico, it is guided by the earth's magnetic fields. My father's telephone is the magnet. Every time you answer my call I get a little nearer to him and you get a little nearer to me. If you want to stay away, don't answer the phone.

Pause.

Are you still there Bennet?

Pause.

Hello?

Pause.

Bennet?

Pause.

Bennet   I'm still here.

Lavelli's Daughter   You know, it's strange. It is women who tell me I am beautiful, not men. It is women who watch me very carefully, not men. Do you look at your wife, Bennet? Pick a blue flower. The little blue flower is favoured by men in love.

Theatre Scene 8

Bennet *carries a blue flower. Walks to his wife. She avoids looking at him.*

Bennet   I've bought you a flower. The little blue flower is favoured by men in love.

Bennet's Wife   Turn your face away.

Bennet   Why?

Bennet's Wife   Your breath smells of meat.

Pause.

You caught the skin disease from him.
It's the same.

Bennet   The same as what?

Bennet's Wife   The Italian. He has that on his forehead. Exactly the same.

Bennet   The Italian is dead.

Bennet's Wife   Last night Mr Lavelli spoke to me. He said he falls down a lot but he had found a way of falling without hurting himself. He said he lets his body relax into the floor.

A horrified **Bennet** *and his young wife stare at the floor. A follow spot becomes their gaze. Searching for* **Lavelli** *as if he had the ability to integrate with floorboards.*

Film Scene 4

Interior. Car.
Camera moves between **Bennet**'s *face and* **Lavelli**'s *face.*
Bennet *stabs* **Lavelli** *in the stomach.*
Bennet *looks at his watch.*
Blood pours out of **Lavelli**'s *nose and drips on to his salami roll.*

Exterior. Car.
Bennet *opens passenger door.* **Lavelli**'s *body falls out of the car. As he falls,* **Lavelli**'s *mobile phone falls out of his pocket. It begins to ring.* **Bennet** *looks at it. Eventually, he answers it.*

Bennet   Hello. Who is this? I don't know who I'm speaking to. No this is Bennet answering for Senor Lavelli. Who is speaking? Who? His daughter? Yes, we had a good meeting. Thank you. I have just driven your father to the airport. He is flying to Rome in twelve minutes. Unfortunately, he has left his phone in my car. What would you like me to do with it?

Bennet *notices something strange. Three butterflies circle the corpse. He puts his hand to his forehead.* **Bennet** *seems to have caught* **Lavelli**'s *eczema in the shape of a number three.*

Bennet   Sorry I didn't hear what you said?

He bites into **Lavelli**'s *bloody salami roll. Chews with gusto.*

Theatre Scene 9

Lavelli's *ghost watches* **Bennet's Wife** *eat a sandwich. She wears a tall coiffed blonde wig.*

Lavelli   The blonde must appear to be flighty. We want to peel off her mask in the same way we want to pin down a butterfly and study the fragile creature who evades us. A naked blonde clutching a sheet against her breasts imitates a crumbling man's dream. He wants to feel he can pin her to the sheet. And she must never have an appetite.

Bennet *enters. Watches his wife drop the sandwich from her hand.*

Bennet Are you asleep?

Bennet's Wife Yes.

Bennet Are you crying?

Bennet's Wife No.

Bennet Are you frightened?

Bennet's Wife No.

Bennet Are you happy to live your life with me?

Bennet's Wife Yes.

Bennet Are you lying?

Bennet's Wife Wash your hands before you touch me.

Bennet Why?

Bennet's Wife I can smell your car.

His mobile starts ringing.

Answer your phone.

Film Scene 5

Interior. Restaurant.
Waiter *unwraps the present* **Lavelli** *gave him. It is an oriental ivory haircomb in the shape of a butterfly. He unties his long black glossy hair which has been scraped into a bun. It ripples down his back.* **Waiter** *combs his lustrous mane with the oriental ivory butterfly.*

Theatre Scene 10

The lights find **Bennet**. *A mobile hugged to his ear. He eats a Mars Bar.*

Bennet   I don't want to talk.

Lavelli's Daughter (*voice-over*)   Bennet, I have telephoned the airline. They say my father was not on the plane. Tomorrow I will call the police. But something good has happened. Last night a Polish man I admire very much took me to the theatre. Afterwards we drank rum and grapefruit juice and then he looked nervous. He said there were butterflies in his stomach. I am in love. Yes, after all this time I am in love. Bennet, when you drove my father to the airport, what did he talk about?

Bennet   He told me to take a sauna.

Lavelli's Daughter   Why is that, Bennet?

Bennet   He said the heat would be good for my stiff English spine.

He stuffs his mouth with chocolate.

Lavelli's Daughter   Anything else?

Bennet   He had eczema on his forehead.

Lavelli's Daughter   So my father was anxious?

Pause.

Are you still there?

Bennet   Yes, I'm still here.

Lavelli's Daughter   His skin disease was a memory. He abandoned his daughter and she is very angry. My father knew this. It takes a lot of energy to run away from someone's anger.

Bennet Where are you?

Lavelli's Daughter The man I am in love with is shy, uncertain. Like me he doesn't know what to make of the situation. I am walking to his apartment in Trastevere. This is my favourite part of Rome. It is like a village. I have just walked past the church of Santa Cecilia. She is our patron saint of music because she sang in her bath while her head was hacked off with an axe. Do you think he is in love with me, Bennet? When you are lonely you sometimes misjudge these things. What do you think?

Bennet I can't hear you. You keep fading out.

Lavelli's Daughter Return to your wife. Do not give her a rose. Roses that bloom beyond their proper season foretell death.

Theatre Scene 11

Bennet's Wife *has grown taller. She wears very high shoes.*

Bennet's Wife Can you see him?

Bennet No.

Lavelli's *ghost parts his hair and shows eczema mark in shape of number 3.*

Bennet's Wife He is showing me his skin disease. I can see it on you.

Bennet (*touching his forehead*) I can't feel anything.

Bennet's Wife He says dying is easy. The clever thing is to know how to make people disappear.

Bennet (*whispers*)   Senor Lavelli is dead.

Lavelli (*to* **Bennet's Wife**)   Tell him as a child I was famous for my ability to mimic sticks. Yes! I was like a caterpillar who freezes his body at right angles when a predator threatens!

Bennet's Wife   He says to tell you that as a child he was famous for mimicking sticks.

Lavelli   The caterpillar is very good at playing dead.

Bennet's Wife   He says the caterpillar is very good at playing dead.

Bennet *looks at her, astonished.*

Bennet's Wife   Am I still your wife?

Bennet   Yes. Of course you are still my wife.

Kisses the top of her immaculate hair.

You are the woman of my dreams.

Bennet's Wife (*flat*)   Don't put your face next to mine.

Her face is held away from **Bennet** *so that she looks absurdly uncomfortable.*

His skin disease is in you. Keep your face turned. I can think you into me.

Bennet   No you can't.

Bennet's Wife   He says I can think your dream into me and become it.

Bennet   Eczema is not infectious.

Lavelli   Everything is infectious. If I am impolite to you, you are impolite to me.

Bennet's Wife   He says everything is infectious.

Bennet's *mobile rings.*

Bennet   He is dead.

Bennet's Wife   But he hasn't disappeared.

Bennet   And his daughter is looking for him.

Fade in film:
Exterior. Woods.
The three five-year-old **Girls** *stare unblinkingly from the screen.*
Bennet *stares at them.*

Italian five-year-old **Girl** (*sings*)   Domani Domani Domani.

She holds a bunch of dying roses in her hand.

All Girls (*sing*)   Tomorrow Tomorrow Tomorrow.

Theatre Scene 12

Lights find **Bennet**. *Mobile hugged to his ear. A wilting rose sits in the button hole of his pinstriped suit. He is eating chocolate.*

Lavelli's Daughter (*voice-over*)   Bennet? I am walking up the stairs to my new lover's apartment. He has five pink geraniums in a pot outside his door. I feel very nervous. It is so long since I have touched a man. My cheeks burn every time he is near me.

Pause.

Bennet   You said it is a long time since you touched a man.

Lavelli's Daughter   Bennet, when my boyfriend took me to the theatre I removed my spectacles. I could not see anything but I think it helped him see me. If you ever want to be invisible, wear spectacles. What do you think has happened to my father? Sorry? I can't hear you?

Film Scene 6

Exterior. A small suburban garden.
Bennet *and* **Bennet's Wife** *finish digging over a grave.*
Lavelli's *shoes and cashmere coat are placed to one side.*
Bennet's Wife *is breathless. She leans on a spade. Flushed.
There is blood on her hands. She drinks from a bottle of Evian
water.*
Film fades.

Lavelli's Daughter (*voice-over*)   Bennet, I feel like I am
alive again. I think I have been dead all these years.
When you are lonely it is like living at the end of the
world. I'm taking off my dress in the bedroom. It is a
blue dress. Now I am in my underwear. My brassiere is
too small for my breasts. Now he's walking towards me.

She walks on to the stage carrying a suitcase and mobile phone.

He is taking off my pants. His fingers are cold.
(*Whispers.*) Oh God, Bennet, I have not washed my pants
since my father died. I know they are not clean. But if I
move my legs just so he won't see . . . Bennet, he is
kissing the inside of my thighs . . . oh . . . oh . . . he is
moving down . . . my pants are on the floor, thank God
. . . I think I peed in them . . . just a little. He has his
tongue inside me . . . I hope you don't mind me telling
you this?
(*Erotic bliss.*) Oh oh oh.
Tomorrow we go to Warsaw . . . Bennet . . . his hand is
on my breast now, oh oh, Bennet, I'm having sex for
the first time in two years . . . he is thrusting into me
. . . oh, Bennet, I am so confused . . . is the waiter that
last saw my father called Michael or Tan? Hello? I can't
hear you.

Film Scene 7

Interior. Restaurant.
Close-up of **Waiter**'s *face. Tears stream down his cheeks. His
long hair is scraped back into a bun which is secured by the
oriental ivory butterfly comb. He is speaking to* **Lavelli's
Daughter** *on a mobile phone.* **Lavelli's Daughter** *asks
questions on stage but we see* **Waiter** *on film.*

Waiter   My name is Tan. But in my passport it says
Michael.

Lavelli's Daughter   You knew my father. Did you
like him or did something happen between you?

Waiter   No! I liked him very much. There was no bad
feeling between myself and your father.

Lavelli's Daughter   Were you friends?

Waiter   Yes.

Lavelli's Daughter   Were you intimate friends?

Waiter   Yes. We were lovers.

Lavelli's Daughter   Where was he going when you
last saw him?

Waiter   He was returning to Rome.

Lavelli's Daughter   Was it a casual affair?

Waiter   No. We wanted to see each other again.

Lavelli's Daughter   So, you were the last person he
saw?

Waiter   The last person he saw was his business
partner. I don't know his name.

Lavelli's Daughter   Did he ever speak about me?
About his family?

Waiter   I knew he was married. His wife died two
years ago. Yes, he spoke about you. He said you always
ask him when he is coming to see you?

Lavelli's Daughter   That's not me.

Waiter   Pardon?

Lavelli's Daughter   He has two daughters. My sister is five years old.

Waiter   I didn't know he has another daughter. He has a five-year-old daughter?

Lavelli's Daughter   Yes, Flavia.

Waiter   Flavia?
Hello?
Are you there?
Hello?

We see **Bennet** *sitting at a table nearby. He is wearing spectacles.*

Theatre Scene 13

Bennet's Wife *stands centre stage.*
She has her back to us. She wears a red dress. Combs her long golden hair which trails down her back. She wears a diamanté tiara and long gloves. She is coming into focus now as a screen goddess.

An identical woman enters. She too wears a red dress. She too has long golden hair. There is no doubt that she too is **Bennet's Wife**. *She speaks.*

Woman (*flat*)   In my dream my mother is dressed as a prawn, and the prawn is wearing a Bette Davis hat, her round black eyes at the side of her head, and she says: 'You are just a little version of me.'

The impostor with her back to us, turns round. It is **Lavelli** *dressed as Bennet's Wife.*

Lavelli   You are just a little version of me.

Bennet's Wife *screams.*
Lavelli *imitates her scream.*

Lavelli   No. That is not absolutely right. A bad
forgery. I try again.

He imitates her scream with more volume.

It is difficult to become you.

He circles her.

Difficult because you have not yet become you. You
have no centre for me to excavate in my mimicry. I can
only imitate your surface. For this I am grateful. I do
not have enough terror in my throat to make a good
forgery of what is inside you.

Bennet's Wife (*flat*)   Tired. I am so tired.

Lavelli's Daughter *crosses the stage with suitcase.*

Bennet's Wife   The sound of waking birds. Three
pillows. Sometimes four. The light on. Always a glass of
water. In case of choking. The radio on. Late-night
radio. A low time. Six blankets. Silence, but not really.
(*Whispers.*) A water pipe. The floor creaking. My
husband's breath.

Lavelli *screams. His scream makes her scream.*

Lavelli (*brushes his suit*)   Only a spider.
Why are you screaming?

Bennet's Wife (*flat*)   Something happened to me.

Pause.

But I can't remember.

Pause.

I've forgotten.

Bennet's Wife *starts to breathe in and out as if in a panic.*

Lavelli *starts to breathe in and out as if in a panic.*
They stop.

Bennet's Wife (*flat*)   I know how ... I know how ...
ta ta tender it is ta ta to love ... to love the ... to
love ...

Lavelli   Try again.

Bennet's Wife (*flat*)   I know how tender it is to love
... to love the ... to love the bah bah ... to ... to ...
love ...

Pause.

Lavelli (*prompting*)   To love ...

Bennet's Wife   To love to love to love the bah bah
to love love love the –

Lavelli   Your mother said, I have given suck, and
know how tender 'tis to love the babe that milks me.

Bennet's Wife (*flat*)   I have given suck, and know
how tender it is to love the babe that milks me. I would
while it was sma sma ...

Lavelli   I would while it was smiling in my face –

Bennet's Wife (*flat*)   I would while it was smiling in
my face ... pla pla pla –

Lavelli   Pluck my nipple from its boneless gums –

Bennet's Wife (*flat*)   Pluck my nipple from its
boneless gums –

Lavelli   And dash the brains out.

Bennet's Wife (*flat*)   And dash the brains out.

Lavelli   Oh oh oh.

Bennet's Wife (*flat*)   Oh oh oh.

Lavelli   And then she killed herself.

Bennet's Wife (*flat*)   And then she killed herself.

Pause.

She starts to sob.
Lavelli *imitates her sob.*
Enter **Bennet**. *He watches her sob.*

Bennet's Wife (*softly murderous*)   Tell her you promise you'll always answer her calls.

Bennet   I don't want to speak to her.

Lavelli   You walk to your husband and you say, Great Glamis, worthy Cawdor.

Bennet's Wife (*flat*)   Great Glamis, worthy Cawdor.

Bennet (*smiles, and then laughs*)   Is the heating on?

Bennet's Wife   It's always on.

He hands her a parcel wrapped in tissue paper.

Bennet   A present.

Bennet's Wife   What is it?

Lavelli   A butterfly.

She opens it. Takes out an oriental ivory hair comb.

Bennet   A butterfly.

He takes the comb from her. Tenderly combs her long golden hair. His mobile phone rings.

Bennet's Wife (*to* **Lavelli**'s *ghost*)   Tell your daughter that my eyes are open when in truth the window is shut and the curtains drawn. Tell your daughter I have lengthened my limbs and that I have not forgotten to breathe. Tell your daughter that if she looks at me she'll die.

Lights find **Lavelli's Daughter** *with suitcase.*
Bennet *puts his mobile to his wife's ear.*

Lavelli's Daughter   Allow me to recommend to you
an Italian liqueur for the end of your meal. Amaro
Averna . . . from Sicilia. But that is not where I am.
Sicilia, I mean. I'm on the move all the time. Business. I
am in fact very close, Bennet. I am on my way to see
you. And your wife. Is it true what my father said? That
all English gardens look like graveyards?

Film Scene 8

Interior. Restaurant.
Waiter *sits at table. He wears his hair in a bun, secured by the
ivory butterfly comb.*
Bennet *sits with him. He wears spectacles. He is talking.*
But there is no sound.
Bennet *sips an espresso. Swallows pills.*
Bennet *puts his hand provocatively into* **Waiter***'s hair.*
Takes out the butterfly comb.
There is something erotic in this action.
Waiter*'s hair falls to his shoulders.*
Bennet *fondles the glossy black hair.*
He then grasps **Waiter** *by the neck.*
He might be about to kiss him.
Instead, **Bennet** *strangles* **Waiter** *with all his strength.*
Fade film.

Theatre Scene 14

Lavelli*'s ghost surveys* **Bennet's Wife***. She wears glittering
diamanté earrings.*

Lavelli   Walk into the light.

She does so.

Open your eyes.

She does so.

Stare out into the middle distance.

She does so.

Bring your hands together as if you are washing them.

She does so.

Say after me (*Thick Italian.*), all the perfumes of Arabia will not sweeten this leetle hand. Oh! Oh! Oh!

Bennet's Wife   All the perfumes of Arabia will not sweeten this little hand. Oh! Oh! Oh!

Lavelli   Yes, not a bad forgery. Oh! Oh! Oh!

Theatre Scene 15

Bennet *holds his mobile phone to his ear. A white feather nestles in the top pocket of his pinstriped suit.* **Lavelli's Daughter** *takes a seductive dress out of her suitcase. Takes off her red dress, puts it in suitcase and struggles into new dress while she speaks.*

Lavelli's Daughter (*voice-over*)   Strong coffee in the morning makes me want to shit . . . but I don't want to because the only toilet here – I'm in southern Europe now, Bennet . . . won't be long before we meet – the only toilet here in this village is a stinking hole swarming with flies and the window is open so that I can smell the crate of sardine guts waiting to be collected by the garbage men . . . I don't know what to do, Bennet . . . I just gotta . . . I gotta shit my stomach hurts . . . I don't want to squat over this hole . . . oh . . . God . . . oh . . . I'm . . . I'm (*Weep.*) missing my father. That's why I'm talking to you, what do you think happened to him, Bennet?

Bennet   Where in Europe are you?

Lavelli's Daughter   Two hours away by aeroplane. I will see you tomorrow.

Bennet   Tomorrow?

Lavelli's Daughter   Yes. Tomorrow. Return to your wife. If you see a white bird shut your eyes. White birds are a sign of death.

Theatre Scene 16

Bennet *strokes his wife's back with a white feather.*

Bennet   Do you love me?

Bennet's Wife   Yes.

Bennet   Are you asleep?

Bennet's Wife   Yes.

Bennet   Are you looking forward to tomorrow?

Bennet's Wife   Yes.

Bennet   Do you know why you love me?

Bennet's Wife   Yes.

Bennet   Do you know why I love you?

Bennet's Wife   Yes.

His mobile phone rings.

Don't answer it.

Bennet   I promised.

Bennet's Wife   Break your promise.

Bennet   I can't.

Bennet's Wife   Look at me.

Bennet   I look at you all the time.

Bennet's Wife She is very close.

Bennet Yes.

Bennet's Wife So there is no need to take her call.

Bennet (*answering phone*) Hello.

Lavelli's Daughter (*voice-over*) Did you know my father has another daughter? From a woman he saw while he was married to my mother. My stepsister is called Flavia. She's five years old. When she stood up for the first time my father said this is a very old world. To think there must have been a small girl in the Stone Age who tried to do the same thing.

Bennet Where is she?

Lavelli's Daughter I don't know.

Fade in film:
Exterior. Woods.
Three five-year-old **Girls** *stare unblinkingly from the screen. They wear Elizabethan costumes and hairstyles. The three* **Girls** *open their mouths but no sound comes out. They are mouthing the word 'tomorrow'.*

Bennet Where are you?

Lavelli's Daughter I am standing outside your house.

Bennet *and* **Bennet's Wife** *exchange looks.*

Theatre Scene 17

Lavelli's Daughter *carries a suitcase.*
She shakes hands with **Bennet's Wife**.
Bennet *stands near her.*

Lavelli's Daughter I hope you don't have a dog. Dogs are like a demented mind . . . they follow you about and watch you.

Lavelli *enters.*

Lavelli (*to* **Bennet's Wife**)   To welcome my daughter you say *piacere.*

Bennet's Wife   *Piacere.*

Lavelli's Daughter   I am pleased to meet you.

Lavelli   And then you offer her a drink. *Ti posso offrire una bevanda?*

Bennet's Wife   *Ti posso offrire una bevanda?*

Lavelli's Daughter   I have some champagne in my bag. Do you have any children?

Lavelli   No, *non ho bambini.*

Bennet's Wife   No, *non ho bambini.*

Lavelli's Daughter   Your wife speaks such good Italian.

Bennet   You are very welcome.

Lavelli   A good hostess says, let me take your bag.

Bennet's Wife   Let me take your bag.

Lavelli's Daughter *gives* **Bennet's Wife** *her suitcase.*

Lavelli's Daughter   May I see your garden? (*To* **Bennet's Wife**.) *Giardino.*

Film Scene 9

Exterior. Suburban garden.
Bennet *and* **Lavelli's Daughter** *stand on the small square of grass.*
Lavelli's Daughter's *attention is taken by something.*
Bennet *follows her gaze.*

Three butterflies hover above a mound of earth.
This is where **Lavelli***'s body is buried.*

Theatre Scene 18 *(same time as previous film scene)*

Bennet's Wife *opens* **Lavelli's Daughter***'s suitcase.*
Takes out the dress **Lavelli's Daughter** *has worn throughout.*
Rolled inside it is a gun. She puts it to one side. Slips
Lavelli's Daughter*'s dress on.* **Lavelli** *enters and watches*
her.

Bennet's Wife *(flat)* I'm becoming sad, disconnected
from intimate pleasure . . . my father was the only
person to see this, 'It's in your hands,' he said before he
left Rome, 'your fingers are cold.' He said that in
England people are kind and that all English gardens
looks like graveyards.

Lavelli   Yes. Not a bad forgery. But it lacks a leetle
something! You do not have the Mediterranean sun in
your body. And you do not have love in your body. So
now you must move as if the sunshine is slowing you
down.

Theatre Scene 19

Lavelli's Daughter   My lover let me down, Bennet.
I'm in a bad mood. He said to me, 'I can't move in
with you. I have these feelings of ambivalence. It might
not work out. I can't get a picture of the future. I am
full of fear every day.' But that's what the future is, isn't
it, Bennet? The future is unknown.

Bennet   Not necessarily.

Lavelli's Daughter   I want to get a picture of my
father's last days.

Pause.

And you have caught his eczema.

She feels his forehead.

Bennet   My wife won't touch me.

Lavelli's Daughter *traces the eczema in the shape of a 3 with her finger.*

Lavelli's Daughter   Why should your wife touch you when you can't feel anything?

Bennet   I can feel you.

Lavelli's Daughter   Why is that, Bennet?

Bennet   Because you want to hurt me.

Lavelli's Daughter   You can feel that?

Bennet   Yes. It gets through.

Lavelli's Daughter   Why do you think my father was so distressed when he was with you?

Bennet   He was happy. He talked about butterflies.

Lavelli's Daughter   But the mark on his forehead.

Bennet   He said he got the disease because he feels too much.
He was in his favourite restaurant. I think he was feeling . . . the waiter.

Pause.

He was happy. He couldn't stop smiling.

Lavelli's Daughter   I know my father slept with men. He told me.

Bennet's Wife *enters.* **Lavelli***'s ghost follows.*

Lavelli's Daughter   Is your wife asleep?

Bennet Of course.

Lavelli's Daughter Why is she wearing my dress?

Bennet Ask her.

Lavelli's Daughter Why is she wearing my clothes?

Bennet's Wife Look at me.

Lavelli No. You must never plead for attention. It is better to say don't look at me. Your dream is to be noticed. But what is it you want to be regarded for? You want to be looked at but you do not know how you want to be looked at. A gaze of terror will do. You want to see panic in my daughter's eyes. Your mother pulled you from her breast. She killed herself. Your blonde head is still pressed against the wall. Remember, you cannot murder without terror . . . so use what you have inside you . . .

Bennet's Wife May I sit with my husband?

Lavelli No. It is better to stand if you want to be looked at.

Lavelli's Daughter Why does your wife talk to my father in her sleep?

Bennet Ask her.

Bennet's Wife (*takes out gun and points it at* **Lavelli's Daughter**) I talk to your father because he is training me to be your assassin.

Lavelli There are no bullets in my daughter's gun. She carries it because it makes her feel safe.

Lavelli's Daughter Is your wife still asleep?

Bennet My wife is asleep.

Bennet's Wife *walks slowly towards* **Lavelli's Daughter** *pointing the gun.*

Bennet's Wife   The sunshine is slowing me down. I can feel it in my body.

Lavelli's Daughter   But it is night.

Bennet's Wife (*walking like a screen goddess towards her prey*)   Last night a man I admire very much arrived at my apartment. We drank rum and grapefruit juice and then he looked nervous. He said there were butterflies in his stomach. I am in love. Yes, after all this time I am in love. How is it that I have ended up so very solo, Bennet? I have no lover, no garden, no child.

She takes hold of **Lavelli's Daughter**. *Bangs her head violently against something while she speaks.*

You know it's strange. It is women who tell me I am beautiful, not men. It is women who watch me very carefully, not men. Do you look at your wife, Bennet? On your way home pick a blue flower. The little blue flower is favoured by men in love.

This is **Bennet**'s *cue. He leans towards* **Lavelli's Daughter** *as if he is going to kiss her. Instead, he strangles her. His wife turns to* **Lavelli**.

Bennet's Wife (*soft, sarcastic*)   The blonde must appear to be flighty. We want to peel off her mask in the same way we want to pin down a butterfly and study the fragile creatures who evades us.

Pause.

I want a cup of tea.

Film Scene 10

Exterior. Small suburban garden.
Bennet *has just finished digging over another grave. We, of course, know they have buried* **Lavelli's Daughter**.
Bennet's Wife *drinks a bottle of Evian water like she is dying of thirst.* **Bennet** *buries his mobile phone in the earth.*

Theatre Scene 20

Bennet *slumps with a cup of tea.*
Bennet's Wife *sleeps standing up in her nightdress. She holds some sugar lumps in her hand.*

An atmosphere of inertia, heat, nausea.

We hear the ghostly amplified voices of **Lavelli** *and* **Lavelli's Daughter**'s *ghosts − but we do not see them. Everything is very still.*

Lavelli   A leetle information. Sugar is poison.

Lavelli's Daughter (*in Italian*)   Zucchero e veleno.

Bennet   Is the heating on?

Lavelli   The German scholar − Doctor Rauwolf, who practised in 1573 − noted that when the Turks and Moors discovered sugar they were no longer intrepid soldiers.

Bennet's Wife   The heating is always on.

Bennet *drops another sugar lump into his tea.*

Lavelli   If I was his zookeeper I would feed him chocolate mousse made with sixty per cent cocoa . . . a leetle splash of rum . . . but no sugar . . .

Bennet *puts his hand to his throat. It feels chilled. Puts his hand to his head. It feels heavy.*

Lavelli   It is easy to murder. But it is difficult to give up sugar.

Lavelli's Daughter   Before you died, you were thinking of Flavia.
Lavelli   Yes.

Lavelli's Daughter   You were not thinking of me.

Lavelli   No.

Lavelli's Daughter   For you I was already dead?

Lavelli   Yes.

Lavelli's Daughter   You knew he would find me.

Lavelli   Yes.

Bennet *takes another sugar lump.*

Lavelli's Daughter   You were thinking how your youngest daughter said, 'When are you coming to Pisa?'

Lavelli   Yes.

Lavelli's Daughter   And you said, tomorrow.

Lavelli   I said tomorrow. I am coming to Pisa tomorrow.

Bennet *puts his hand to his head.*

Lavelli's Daughter (*in Italian*)   Vengo a Pisa domani.

Lavelli   I broke my promise.

Bennet's Wife   I can smell something on your breath.

Lavelli's Daughter   Nausea.

Lavelli (*in Italian*)   Si, nausea.

Bennet's Wife (*very faint*)   Vomit.

Bennet *takes another sugar lump.*

Lavelli   Flavia is a memory that is inside me, and outside me. A memory written on my forehead in scabs.

Lavelli's Daughter   He caught your memory.

Lavelli   Yes. He caught my memory.

Pause.

Lavelli   Before I died, I was thinking that tomorrow is a promise that is always broken.

Fade in film:
Three five-year-old **Girls** *stare unblinkingly from the screen.*

Lavelli's five-year-old (*sings*)
    'Domani Domani Domani'

And then she fires a gun. The same gun **Bennet's Wife** *unpacked from the suitcase.*
Bennet *puts his hand to his head. Massages his forehead. Lights fade.*

End.